User Fees

# USER FEES

## A Practical Perspective

Miriam A. Drake
Assistant Director
Libraries and Audio-Visual Center
Purdue University

Libraries Unlimited, Inc.
Littleton, Colorado
1981

LIBRARIES UNLIMITED, INC.
P.O. Box 263
Littleton, Colorado 80160

---

**Library of Congress Cataloging in Publication Data**

Main entry under title:

User fees.

    Bibliography: p. 137
    Includes index.
    Contents: Fee for service in libraries /
Miriam A. Drake -- The allocation of resources /
Richard L. Pfister -- What's a nice librarian like
you doing behind a cash register? / Fay M.
Blake -- [etc.]
    1. Libraries--Fees--Addresses, essays, lectures.
I. Drake, Miriam A.
Z683.U84       025.5'24       81-6032
ISBN 0-87287-244-0       AACR2

# PREFACE

The subject of user fees in libraries is a contentious and emotional issue.  The availability of computer-based services from commercial firms, which has accelerated the costs of library oper- ations, and the efforts to reduce local property taxes and library funding have caused librarians, governing boards, and municipal officials to consider new and different methods of financing library services.  Several methods have been and will continue to be explored in an effort to make library services available to the people who want and need them.  This book contains papers dealing with one method of funding those services:  user fees.

Four of the papers included here were prepared for a workshop on user fees sponsored by the Indiana Chapter of the Special Libraries Association.  In the first of these, Richard Pfister boldly reviews the issue from the perspective of an economist concerned with the allocation of resources--the library's, the institution's, the society's, and the individual's.  In the second workshop paper, Fay Blake expresses the concern of many public librarians, that user fees limit access to information for those who simply cannot pay.  Sandra Rouse brings to this volume the results of surveys conducted at Univer- sity of Illinois with regard to on-line reference services at the Big Ten university libraries.  The fourth of the papers that were prepared for the workshop was written from the perspective of the corporate librarian.  This paper was prepared by Faye Brill, who has worked in two types of corporate setting.

Since these papers contain views and ideas not previously made available to the profession, it was decided to combine them with other materials, written by professionals working in a wide variety of situations, to produce a publication with broad coverage of the subject.  In addition to my own overview, the article by Jack Key and Katherine Sholtz was prepared especially for this volume.  Their essay provides a unique view of the effect user fees have had upon the clients of a medical library, specifically that of the Mayo Clinic.

The remaining articles in this volume--those by Roger Stoakley, Deputy County Librarian of West Sussex, England; Grieg Aspnes, a special librarian serving industry; Nancy Kingman and Carol Vantine, of the 3M Library and the Minneapolis Public Library respectively, both of which are subscribers to INFORM, a fee-based information service; Oscar Firschein, Roger Summit, and Colin Mick, all of whom work with research facilities in California; and James Dodd, whose work at the Georgia Institute of Technology has involved dealing with independent information brokers--provide even more diverse views and perspectives upon the volatile subject of user fees.  It is hoped that making this diversity of approaches available to the profession will further discussion of the issue and lead to informed and considered

5

decisions in those institutions faced with the problem of changing sources of library funding.

I want to thank all the authors whose work is included in this book for their significant contributions. Special thanks is due the authors of the original papers for their patience and help and to the Board of Directors of the Indiana Chapter, Special Libraries Association for their help and support.

Miriam A. Drake
West Lafayette, Indiana
February 1981

# TABLE OF CONTENTS

FEES FOR SERVICE THROUGH INFORMATION BROKERS

BIBLIOGRAPHY

# INTRODUCTION

The financial plight of libraries in the United States has been the subject of news stories and discussion for several years. The prices paid by libraries for books and journals have risen at a higher rate than prices of most goods and services. Library budgets, already squeezed by inflation, have been further burdened by the necessity of providing a growing variety of computer-based bibliographic and source information services. Library funders in the public sector have not been able to raise sufficient amounts of tax funds to support existing collections and services, and funds for new programs are not available to most public libraries. Librarians, local, county, and state officials, and college and university administrators have had to look to alternative sources of funding. While some libraries have been successful in attracting grants and endowments and others have received gifts from Friends of the Library and other groups, many have had to turn to user fees or fees for special services in order to obtain funds sufficient to meet users' demands. Generally, user fees are implemented as a last resort. In many instances, the user has a choice of performing a time-consuming manual search at no direct charge or a faster, and often more exhaustive, computer-based search for a fee. The user's decision will be based on experience, urgency of need, and the value of his/her time. Users are often wary of the results of computer-based searching and feel more comfortable with familiar techniques, regardless of the time involved. Others feel that the value of their time far outweighs the cost of using computer-based systems.

The views expressed by librarians in conferences and in the literature vary widely, and many find themselves in the middle. They want to provide appropriate and responsive service but feel that libraries should not charge for service, although some place computer-based services in a special category and feel it is acceptable to charge for these services, provided that the user has a choice.

This book provides a sampling of views and librarians' experiences with user fees. Many excellent articles have been written that could not be included in this volume. These articles are cited in the Bibliography; the reader should give special attention to the two articles written by Marilyn Gell.

## Review of the Issues

The book is divided into six sections, each dealing with a different aspect of or experience with user fees. The two papers in the first section, Review of the Issues, are focused on the economics of libraries and the economic aspects of public policy concerning libraries. My own review raises questions about who pays and who should pay in the context of inflation, declining availability of funds

for libraries, technology, public policy, and library usage. There is
little doubt in my mind that library services in the future will not be
the same as they are today. The role of libraries in schools, communities, colleges and universities, and corporations will be affected significantly by client needs, by government finances, by technology that
brings information directly to the home and office, and by energy
availability. Some libraries will thrive by offering a variety of
services to a public recognizing the need and desirability of these
services. Since libraries are not monolithic institutions, we can
expect their roles to differ, depending on their institutional environments, as well as on their clientele's demands and willingness to
pay either directly through fees, indirectly through taxes, or through
a combination of financing methods.

In the second article of the first section, Richard Pfister, an
economist, approaches user fees in the context of the allocation of
individual, institutional and societal resources. He raises the issue
of cost/benefit to society and indicates the difficulty of arriving at
a satisfactory conclusion. While data on library budgets are readily
available, data on library costs are scarce. Neither economists nor
librarians have been able to construct the costs curves used by economists. Quantitative benefit data are simply not available; policy
makers must rely on qualitative statements of benefits from library
users. It is not possible to say that one dollar of library cost will
produce X dollars of benefit. There is no doubt that library service
produces public benefit, but this benefit cannot be related to cost in
a simple formula.

Librarians and citizens concerned with libraries should keep in
mind the distinction between the economist's definition of "public
goods" as explained by Pfister, and what is good for the public.
Government programs in all areas may produce benefit for the public
but may not meet the criteria of "public goods."

Pfister also discusses the allocation of resources within the
library emphasizing the need to analyze the cost-effectiveness of
alternative techniques to provide service. Direct charges for service
are suggested as a guide to the library in deciding on the services to
be provided and the allocation of library resources. Pfister's paper
separates the economics of libraries from their social and political
aspects. He suggests techniques for analyzing library service and
makes the critical point that library service will be evaluated by
users and funders, whether objectively or subjectively. He urges
librarians to participate in these evaluation efforts to provide
better guidance to policy makers.

## Opposition Views

As an economist, I agree with Pfister in his assertion that user
fees could bring about more user-responsive service and a more effective allocation of resources. As a librarian and citizen, I share
Fay Blake's concern regarding the availability of information. Blake's
definition of direct fees equates user fees with loan or transaction
fees. It is not clear whether she considers an annual membership fee
to be a user fee. A broader definition would encompass all fees paid

by users directly to the library regardless of the basis. Blake's
fears that user fees will discriminate against the poor and restrict
access to information are shared by many librarians and citizens. In
her search for alternatives to user fees, she has overlooked the idea
of subsidy to individuals who may want library service but who may not
have sufficient funds to pay library fees.

Roger Stoakley also opposes user fees in tax-supported libraries
on the grounds of equity and restriction to access of information. He,
too, views fees in the narrower definition of transaction fees and does
not consider other methods of finance. Stoakley suggests that the
imposition of fees could lead to a requirement that libraries be
self-supporting.

Both Stoakley and Blake express strong opinions in opposition to
fees. Their position is based on the principle that library service
should be free. Neither author fully explores the range of alternatives available to public libraries, and their fear that public
libraries will lose all tax support is unfounded. But they raise
questions important to the debate on user fees and the appropriate
means of funding public libraries. These questions may require new
solutions and should stimulate the reader to reach for the solution
appropriate to the individual library.

## Fees In Public Libraries

The Blake and Stoakley views are not uniform among members of the
library community. Public libraries have been successful in offering
special services to users for a fee. The paper by Grieg Aspnes and
the commentary by Nancy Kingman and Carol Vantine describe INFORM, a
fee-for-service program offered by J.J. Hill Reference Library, the
Minneapolis Public Library, and the University of Minnesota Libraries.
While the Aspnes paper is lengthy, it is worth reading especially for
the comments of INFORM USERS. Librarians can derive many useful ideas
from these users' comments regarding their information needs. The
paper also discusses INFORM's experience and problems. Librarians
considering user fees should become acquainted with INFORM, its users,
and their experiences.

Kingman and Vantine discuss INFORM from a corporate library point
of view. They point out that the business user of libraries wants
accurate information quickly and is willing to pay for it. They also
suggest that the need for an integrated network of information services, based on cooperation and professional demand, is real.

In the last paper of this section, Oscar Firschein, Roger Summit,
and Colin Mick describe an experiment in on-line searching in four
public libraries in Northern California. This paper offers guidelines
to public libraries planning such services. These guidelines are
becoming increasingly essential for public libraries as more source and
fact information becomes available on-line. The authors found that
public librarians possess knowledge and skills readily transferable to
the on-line environment. The librarian's skill in negotiating
reference questions and formulating search strategies provides an
appropriate background for making effective use of a variety of on-line

services. Reference librarians will find that on-line reference tools
not only save time but also permit a more personalized service.

The California experiment revealed that the attitudes of the head
reference librarian and library director are crucial to the success of
these services. This finding is significant as it suggests that
management and leadership are critical in formulating positive staff
attitudes about new services. Enthusiasm of library staff in providing
service will help overcome user reluctance to try a new service.

The checklist provided by the authors of this paper is a useful
tool for librarians and managers planning new services. The key questions of purpose, objectives, and support for new services are raised.

## Academic and Special Libraries

Fee for service is more widespread in academic and special
libraries than in public libraries. Large academic libraries performing on-line searches for faculty and sponsored research projects have
found that fees are essential to support the service. In the first
paper of this section, Sandra Rouse reviews fees charged and the use
of on-line searching in the libraries of the Big Ten universities. She
points out that on-line searching produces a bibliography tailored to
individual need. User surveys conducted at Purdue University have
shown consistently that on-line searching is a valuable service.
Repeat usage of the service confirms that users are willing to pay the
necessary fees.

Rouse presents a useful discussion and categorization of costs of
on-line searching. Librarians should examine these costs carefully
before initiating service or a fee schedule.

Rouse found that the use of on-line services has not resulted in
the cancellation of paper copies of abstracts and indexes. Library
budgets cannot absorb the need for increased staff required to fulfill
the increased demand that would be generated if paper copies of indexes
were not available. Rouse suggests that use of data bases by library
clientele could be encouraged if data base producers and vendors
improve the interactive features of their systems. Costs could be
reduced if intermediaries were eliminated.

The activities of the Mayo Clinic Library combine academic,
research, clinical, and resource-sharing services. The library serves
a broad and large constituency directly and indirectly through network
resource sharing. It charges fees for a variety of services and utilizes charge back to Mayo Clinic departments. The fees collected have
contributed to the library budget while moderating abuses of library
service. Within the Mayo Clinic Library fees have helped guide the
allocation of resources, a feature described by Pfister. The unique
mission of the Mayo Clinic, "a private trust for public purposes" is
carried through to the library and its mission, goals and priorities.
In their article, Jack Key and Katherine Sholtz discuss the advantages
and disadvantages of fees for library service within the context of the
educational, research, and clinical missions of the Mayo Clinic. Their
discussion suggests that when fees are charged the clients paying the
fees must feel that their money was well-spent.

The importance of value received is also expressed by Faye Brill, who has had experience with collecting and paying fees in two corporate libraries. Her paper discusses the internal charging schemes used by these corporations as well as the payments made to outside institutions. Brill shares with Key and Sholtz the idea that user fees can help reduce abuse of information and library service. Such abuse is an important consideration in most institutional settings. Brill emphasizes that libraries are part of corporate overhead and do not contribute directly to revenue or profit. Managers in all types of corporate and institutional environments want to keep overhead costs as low as possible.

In discussing corporate willingness to pay for outside information services Brill emphasizes the criteria of timeliness, reliability, and value received. Public and academic libraries providing service to business and industry, whether fee or free, need to be aware of these criteria and that they will be used to evaluate the library's services.

## Information Brokers

Corporations and individuals needing library and information services but not having an in-house library or wanting to use libraries themselves can call on information brokers. Many information brokerage firms have grown from one-person, free lance operations to large companies providing a variety of services. In this last section of the reader, James Dodd describes how these operations began and how they operate. Generally, information brokers are in business for profit. They use libraries, information centers, and other sources to fulfill their clients' requests. Dodd expresses the view that the fees collected by information brokers do not benefit the free libraries they use, and often the real information specialist is in the library supplying the brokers with information.

Survival of brokers, Dodd states, depends on the ability to respond quickly and effectively. Both business people and university faculty involved in sponsored research or consulting need accurate information quickly. One faculty member on the Purdue campus told me, "I'm sure the library has the information I need, but I don't have time to use it." This faculty member uses a free lance librarian whom he pays, to find needed data and documents. Dodd recognizes that institutional library staff cannot respond as quickly as a broker but that they have ambivalent attitudes about brokers. On the one hand, the brokers keep "nuisance clients" away from the library; on the other hand, some library staff are resentful, jealous, or envious. Again, librarians are in the middle. Realizing that a particular service is needed and valued, the librarian is unable to meet the need within the existing budget.

Dodd concludes that information brokers are filling a gap in library and information service. The real question is whether information brokers should use free libraries to do their work.

As indicated earlier, this book does not contain all the significant papers written on user fees. The bibliography contains citations of important articles that should be read. In addition, selected material related to user fees in other fields is included to provide a broader perspective on fees for government services.

January 1981                                    Miriam A. Drake
                                                Purdue University

# REVIEW OF THE ISSUES

# FEE FOR SERVICE IN LIBRARIES:
# WHO PAYS? WHO SHOULD PAY?

by

Miriam A. Drake
Purdue University
Libraries and Audio-Visual Center

Discussions of fee for service in libraries often evoke images of supermarkets, hucksters, and Madison Avenue. Heated debates on the subject often have ignored trends in information technology, economics, and social policy. The main issue to be resolved in the user fee debate is who should pay for library service. Should library services be funded by government through taxes? Should libraries be funded by user fees? Should there be a combination of subsidy and fees? The answers to these questions are not as obvious as in the past. There is evidence that inflation, increasing taxes, and the public's perception of government are leading to the end of the "free lunch" era. The objectives of this paper are: 1) to present the economic, social and technological trends affecting library service, and 2) to provide a framework for discussion of fees with emphasis on public libraries.

At the outset it should be recognized that library and information services are not free. Most commonly, these services are funded through tax revenues with the taxpayers picking up the bill for services used by a portion of the community or taxing district. Unlike museums, hospitals, and religious organizations, which provide service for a fee paid from consumers' disposable income, most public libraries receive little or no revenue directly from the people served. Consumers residing in a community with library service have no choice about paying because the payment is included in their tax bills.

## Free Library Tradition

Some public libraries charge fees for special services, such as interlibrary loan, photocopying, rental collections, and computer-based bibliographic searching. A study by Forecasting International Ltd. indicated, "most resistance to fee introduction is likely to come from the librarians themselves. . . . Librarians tend to insist that libraries are and must remain, traditionally 'free,' despite their acceptance of fines for overdue books, 'new book' rentals and reservation fees."[1]

Taxpayer-funded library service began in the United States when the first free public library opened in Newington, Connecticut in 1787; however, the free public library was the exception until the latter half of the nineteenth century. Prior to that time libraries were financed by the people who used them. In general, libraries were

financed and organized as subscription or proprietary libraries.  The
subscription library, financed by a periodic fee paid by users, sold
services rather than ownership.  The proprietary library involved a
partnership or corporate arrangement whereby users would invest capital
for shares,[2] which were transferable by sale, gift, or bequest.  Shera
points out that, "it became the practice of proprietary libraries to
permit non-proprietor use of books by those annually paying a stipu-
lated fee . . . ."[3]

These libraries generally evolved into taxpayer-supported free
libraries.  The growth of the free public library paralleled the growth
of the concept of free public education.  Libraries were considered
extensions of the public school system with the added values of supplying information as well as intellectual and moral advancement.[4]

The idea of service to the poor and disadvantaged grew out of
Andrew Carnegie's view of the library as a place where the working
masses could uplift themselves equally with the more affluent members
of society.  The need to teach the English language and American cultural values to the immigrants who arrived in the United States in the
late nineteenth and early twentieth centuries gave additional stimu-
lation to the concept of service to the disadvantaged.

This concept has grown in strength, despite data indicating that
the poor and disadvantaged are not the primary users of libraries.
White, in his studies of public library usage, has concluded that over
half of the public library's use is by children and students.  Adult
use is largely by middle and upper class people using the library primarily for recreational reading.

"But the bulk of the library profession apparently chose to ignore
this evidence, until many of them were painfully made aware of it
by the decline of large urban library usage by the flight of the
middle class to the suburbs.  Besides specific efforts to reach
lower income individuals, one response was to claim that the
public library somehow strayed from its original goals and
achievements of serving the poor and that there was a 'golden
age' when the library was catering largely to immigrants, the
poor, etc.  Unfortunately, this does not seem to have been the
case."[5]

Yet recent articles opposing fee for service have relied heavily on
arguments based on the mythical "golden age" to give librarians a cause
and mission, appealing to the American view of equality.  De Gennaro
observes that, "the idea of free public libraries is firmly embedded in
the American tradition and anyone who tries to undermine it will
encounter fierce opposition."[6]  As Ethel Crockett, the State Librarian
of California, states, "anybody should be able to walk in to borrow a
book, ask a reference librarian for help and go away without paying.
It's as American as corn and Kansas and blueberry pie in the summer
time.  It is the reason we are strong as a nation."[7]  Even Blake and
Perlmutter, who acknowledge that libraries are serving basically the
more affluent and privileged, proclaim that, "free and public
libraries . . . which accept their responsibility for serving everyone
with a full range of information they need" can help the poor,

unemployed and disadvantaged. They indicate that service to these special populations may require giving up service to the population currently being well-served and conclude, "the library could become again the people's university we once were for the poor, alien, the illiterate, and the disregarded as well as the source for information to a changing society."[8] The assumptions underlying the concept of service to special groups is that these services have greater social value than the current practice of providing service to the better educated and middle and upper class segments of society. In addition, there is an implied perception that library work directed at uplifting is more satisfying to the librarian than other forms of library and information service.

The National Commission on Libraries and Information Science (NCLIS) has stressed equal opportunity of access to a variety of information services as a national goal for the development of libraries and networks. In its statement of goals for action, the commission states,

"As an ideal, the National Program would strive to eventually provide every individual in the United States with equal opportunity
of access to that part of the total information resources which
will satisfy the individual's educational, working, cultural and
leisure-time needs and interests, regardless of the individual's
location, social or physical condition, or level of intellectual
achievement."[9]

The commission has proposed an ambitious program of local, state, and federal funding to implement this approach as well as a national agency to operate and coordinate the program. It should be stressed that the NCLIS goal is stated as an ideal. As Swanson points out, no one is sure of the meaning of "equal opportunity of access," and asks what kinds of inequalities are to be remedied?[10] Buckman states, "Given the competition for public funds, it is likely that . . . public authori-ties . . . may take the view that free and universal access to a recorded information is unrealistic and that social goals can be achieved without it."[11]

Horn, in her opposition to user fees argues that "access to infor-mation is a fundamental right of a citizen in a democratic society."[12] There is a difference, however, between information obtained at no cost and freedom of information. Horn argues, "If you concede that the right of access to information is essential, then having fees levied which discriminate against those unable to pay creates barriers that negate that right."[13]

Few would oppose Horn's view of the importance of freedom of information in a democratic society, but whether user's fees would create discrimination is not so clear. Every taxpayer is now paying for library services and information regardless of use. One question to be resolved is whether tax revenue is the most appropriate form of funding. A second question needing resolution is whether institutions, that is libraries, or individuals should be subsidized. Some econo-mists would argue that more effective and responsive service would result if libraries were funded exclusively by fees with subsidies

to individuals who could not afford to pay.  The assumption underlying
this approach is that the people paying fees directly will weigh value
received in relation to price and will not purchase inappropriate or
inferior service.

   The imposition of user fees by government agencies is not a new
idea.  Highways, airports, and the U.S. Postal Service are the primary
examples of services provided by government for a fee.  Persons not
driving motor vehicles do not pay the gasoline taxes to fund construction and maintenance of highways.  People using ground transportation do
not pay air ticket taxes or aviation fuel taxes to fund airports and
the air traffic control system.

## Economists' Views

   Government programs and activities are carried out for a variety
of purposes and reasons.  Most programs are funded because they provide social value, services that individuals cannot provide themselves
or services to society as a whole.  Yet politicians, librarians, economists, and citizens hold disparate opinions of the role of government
in our society and the services to be provided by government.  There
are no easy solutions or simple answers to the economic and social
problems inherent in American life.  Political speeches and articles
in the popular press reveal not only the great diversity of political
and social philosophies but also the complexity and inextricability of
social issues.  Further, the solutions proposed by economists often
appear simplistic and devoid of the social and personal values forming
the basis of public policy.  The primary limitation of economic theory
is that it is based on how things ought to be or how things were,
ceteris paribus.  In the real world, things rarely are equal, stable,
or unaltered, but despite its limitations, economic theory provides a
useful analytical tool for examining policy issues in economic terms
and understanding the economic consequences of government policies.

   Services that benefit the public in general, rather than each
person as an individual, are "public goods."  They include a variety
of activities from national defense to mosquito extermination.  All
members of society receive the benefit of public goods.  There is no
way to divide the goods or services, and they cannot be withheld from
people who do not pay.  Samuelson associates public goods with external
consumption effects and divisibility:

   "The benefits from a public or social good unlike those from a
   purely private good, are seen to involve external consumption
   effects on more than one individual.  By contrast, if a good can
   be subdivided so that each part can be competitively sold separately to a different individual, with no external effects on
   others in the group, it isn't a likely candidate for governmental
   activity."[14]

These external effects, or externalities, may result in positive contributions to social well-being or social disbenefits.  Education,
public health, and public transportation are examples of positive

external consumption effects. Air pollution and airport noise are
examples of disbenefits or negative externalities.

Gell defines a public good as, "a commodity exhibiting two essential characteristics: relative efficiency in joint consumption and
relative inefficiency in exclusion."[15] Efficiency in joint consumption
implies that it is less expensive for individuals to consume services
as a group than as individuals. Police and fire protection are
examples of efficiency in joint consumption and inefficiency in
exclusion. Library service also may be more efficiently consumed by
society as a whole because the cost of collecting transaction fees
from individuals may be higher than the cost of providing service from
tax funds.

Then is library service a public good? The answer is yes and no.
Library service is not a pure public good, but it has attributes of
public goods. While it could be argued that the benefits of library
service, especially public library service, are largely private, the
public or social benefit is significant. In some cases this benefit
may result in positive externalities, as in the cases of education and
research. Since these externalities exist, Casper classifies library
service as a quasi public good. Her rationale is that,

"At the heart of most library service is information. Information
is never consumed in the traditional sense; it is used but never
'used up' . . . Once a piece of information comes into existence
it can be used repeatedly without eliminating its possible availability to other users."[16]

Casper's argument is more appropriate in academic and special
libraries where information seeking for productive purposes may be
greater than in public libraries. Gell points out that adults' main
use of public libraries is recreational rather than information
seeking.[17]

## Nature of Library Costs

Efficiency in joint consumption of library service results primarily from the nature of library costs. Approximately two-thirds of
the costs of library operation are fixed costs, which include the cost
of space, utilities, maintenance, insurance, materials, and technical
processing. Funds are expended to perform these functions whether the
library is used or not. In normal circumstances, as library usage
increases the average unit cost of library service declines. In recent
years, it is doubtful that library usage has kept pace with inflation
in fixed costs; therefore the average unit cost is increasing. For
example, Indiana Public Libraries experienced a 5% increase in circulation per registered borrower between 1974 and 1977. During the same
period operating costs per registered borrower increased 57%.[18] The
average cost per circulation increased 52% from $1.21 in 1974 to $1.84
in 1977.

This trend in increasing average unit cost is not likely to change
in the immediate future. Prices for utilities, salaries and wages, and
library materials will continue to rise faster than library usage. The

increased cost of driving, the availability of paperback books, the
delivery of information via cable television and computer systems, and
the proliferation of special magazines will discourage library usage in
the future.  It is likely that libraries will be forced to seek technological solutions and innovative services to reduce costs and
increase library usage.  Computer-based systems will become increasingly necessary for medium-sized and large libraries to reduce labor
costs.  The acquisition of journals and other documents in microform
will reduce the need for space and binding.

## Funding of Public Libraries

Public libraries are funded primarily by local government through
property taxes; 85% of revenues are derived from local government, 13%
from states, and 5% from the federal government.[19]  These revenues are
enhanced by the contributions of gifts, volunteer labor, and volunteer
library boards responsible for library corporate governance, but funds
available for libraries remain dependent upon the proportion of local
and property tax revenues the community commits to library service.
As a result of proposition 13 and similar amendments, the amount of
funds available to local governments for a variety of activities and
projects including libraries has been reduced.  Further, the trend
toward lower taxes is reflected at all levels of government; the
current call for a national constitutional convention is a reflection
of public unwillingness to allow government expenditures and programs
to expand indefinitely.

The International City Management Association's Committee on
Future Horizons indicates, "the era of massive growth in the public
sector is over. . . . All levels of government will need to adapt to
less growth in real resources.  . . . It is an era of the policies of
the shrinking pie."[20]  The study has also predicted that cities will
be charging fees for more services: "The charge for a service 'should
be high enough so that it is used primarily by the people who need it,
and who are willing to pay the price.'"[21]  Accompanying the reduction in
taxes will be an increase in consumers' disposable personal and discretionary income.  Disposable personal income is the amount of money
individuals have after taxes and other obligations are deducted from
their wages and salaries.  Discretionary income is the amount of money
remaining to individuals after paying for the necessities of life.
High discretionary income plus increased leisure time account, in large
part, for the sales of recreational vehicles, boats and yachts, ski
vacations, and books and magazines.  Information also may be purchased
with discretionary income.

The U.S. Bureau of Labor Statistics (BLS), in its forecast of the
economy into the 1990s, indicates that the rate of growth in local
government expenditures will slow substantially while discretionary
personal income will rise slowly.  Disposable personal income grew at
an average annual rate of 9.6% during the 1973-1977 period.  BLS has
projected the average annual rate of growth for 1980-1985 at 9.9 -
10.2%.  State and local personal taxes during the 1973-1977 period grew
at 11.8% per year.  The projected growth rate for 1980-1985 is 7.9 -
9.1%.[22]

State and local government purchases of goods and services are expected to show an annual rate of growth of 2.9% between 1973 and 1980 and 1.0% between 1980 and 1985. State and local government purchases for education are expected to decline at 5% per year between 1980 and 1985 and 8% per year between 1985 and 1990.[23]

These data lead to the conclusion that the amount of money available to libraries will decline. NCLIS has proposed that funding of public libraries be changed to 30% local, 50% state, and 20% federal, but this shift is not likely to occur in the immediate future because of pressures to reduce inflation, unemployment, taxes, and the continuing threat of recession. As the United States moves into the 1980s the state of the economy will be of increasing concern. The lack of productivity increases and of real economic growth may change dramatically the amounts of money collected and spent by government at all levels. Levy argues that the United States has been executing a free lunch policy since 1965;[24] that policy has resulted in increasing rates of inflation and transfers of funds from producers to nonproducers. In the years ahead this situation will be exacerbated by the increasing age of the population. An older population will require more social and medical programs funded by government and an increase in productivity. Other trends affecting the economy include decreasing rates of consumer saving and increasing rates of consumer debt. The decline in consumer saving means a slower rate of capital formation and lower capital investment.

Librarians concerned with service and income redistribution to the poor need to keep in mind the lessons of economic history. Levy summarizes:

"The time has come to remind ourselves that during the last two hundred years, growth of real income per capita - not redistribution of current income from producer to nonproducers - was responsible for the amelioration of poverty and economic distress."[25]

In an age of inflation, recession, and retrenchment in government spending, the NCLIS proposal appears to be naive and out of date. Recent cutbacks in library budgets and service confirm that libraries cannot compete for funds effectively against police and fire protection, national defense, and health programs.

## Public Library Usage

Library funding is closely tied to the composition of a library's clientele, the use of specific library services, and the importance of the library in the community.

White, in reviewing over 50 surveys going back to the 1930s found a consistent pattern of public library use:

"Only 20 - 40% of adults in America (the percentages vary with the questions asked and the time period covered) have been inside a public library in the 3 - 12 months preceding any survey. Further, that 20 - 40% is predominantly composed of middle and upper middle

class, middle to upper income, white collar - professional -
managerial technical, better educated individuals."[26]

The 1979 Gallup Survey found that the typical library user is
18-34 years of age, female, college educated, and living with children
under 18 years of age.[27]  Surveys conducted in 1947 and 1967 indicated
that only small portions of lower income groups used the public
library.[28]  The number using the library was far below their representation on the population.

The conclusion reached by White and the Gallup surveys is that
recreational reading constitutes the primary use of the library by
adults.  The rate of library use for information is not clear.  The
1975 Gallup Survey indicated that 17% of the adult population surveyed
reported using the library very frequently or fairly frequently to
solve an information problem.[29]  While the printed word was the most
common source of information cited in the survey, television, friends,
and relatives also were named as frequently used sources.[30]  As
Giuliano states, "most of the public have little to do with libraries.
As far as information institutions in our society go, libraries are of
minor importance.  Reading is not now, and never was, the way most
people get the information that counts to them."[31]  These statements
are corroborated by a survey of 2,400 adults in New England.  When
asked about information sources used, respondents ranked the library
ninth among a variety of sources.  The library was used for 17% of
information-seeking situations.  Individual experience, friends,
neighbors, and relatives ranked highest as information sources.[32]

In the 1967 Gallup Survey, the most frequently stated reasons for
not using the public library were;  "no interest," "not enough time,"
and "don't read."  Only 6% of public library nonusers indicated the use
of other libraries.[33]  The main reasons given for nonuse of libraries
in the New England study were;  "don't need libraries," "don't think
libraries could help," and "had enough information from other sources."
In 83% of the information situations covered by the study, the library
was not used.[34]

The growth in the availability of paperback books and specialty
magazines has reduced the dependency on library materials by the adult
reading public.  Adults desiring information on gardening, cooking,
nutrition, jogging, medicine, etc. can go to the paperback book store,
the news stand, or the supermarket and buy information at a relatively
low price.  The purchase of reading and informational material no longer
necessitates a special trip to the library or the consumption of extra
gasoline.  Less affluent adults can obtain used paperback books at
Goodwill or Salvation Army stores, garage sales, and used book stores.

The heavy student use of the public library indicates that the
library functions as an adjunct to the education system.  Public attitudes about libraries may be closely tied to attitudes about education.
Gallup has pointed out that, "education . . . has lost some of its
appeal . . . now a skilled worker who did not finish high school can
earn as much as many college graduates . . ."[35]  The 1972 Gallup Survey
on attitudes toward education indicated that 44% of people surveyed
wanted children to pursue education to obtain better jobs and 38% to
make more money or to achieve financial success.[36]

In 1974 the Gallup Survey asked about the public's perception of the features of a good school. Summary answers included "teachers who are interested in their work and in their students," varied curriculum, promotes "respect for authority," modern equipment, small classes, religious training, etc.[37] Libraries were not mentioned in the list.

A further indication of public attitudes about libraries can be derived from the 1979 ALA survey, which asked whether respondents would favor tax increases to cover necessary costs of public libraries or charging the people who used them. The results were 50% opposed to increased taxes and 51% in favor of user fees.[38]

The findings of polls and surveys and the economic and political trends described earlier indicate that taxpayers are unwilling to subsidize a service that benefits only a few. Librarians, legislators, and citizens need to examine these findings as well as the technology of information delivery, which will dramatically change both consumer habits and public library services.

## Emerging Information Technology

The application of current computer and telecommunications technologies could make many public and academic libraries obsolete before the end of the century. Within a very short time it will be possible for consumers to access a variety of information sources through interactive television or computer terminals in their homes or offices. Developments in microelectronics and fiber optics are bringing about drastic reductions in the costs of computing and telecommunications while enhancing their capabilities for the delivery of information where and when it is needed. Poppel has predicted that by the mid-1980s most American families will own or lease some sort of home information center.[39]

The technology now exists for people to access dictionaries, encyclopedias, and fact banks on-line. Electronic newspapers and magazines as well as book lists will be available in the home or office via videotext, which utilizes an adapted television set or a computer terminal. The day is rapidly approaching when information seekers will not need to use the library. People accessing bibliographic data and requiring books, journals, or other documents will need document delivery services but may choose a source other than the library. When the cost of going to the library is added to the value of the user's time in travel and finding the needed material, the cost of document delivery service, via electronics, the mail, or the paperback store, is likely to be less.

"Technology has already evolved to a point where access to most of the world's literature can be obtained within a couple of days through a combination of the on-line bibliographic search utilities and vendor-supplied computerized order fulfillment systems for books, documents and periodical articles."[40]

Information and document delivery to the home or office is being developed largely in the private sector. Small and large companies have seen a market for both general and specialized information services, and librarians generally ha·  not been involved in these developments.

Haywood has observed that library education and training do not equip
librarians to deal with the information industry. He states, "I
believe that our formal library school syllabuses need some radical
revision in the area of 'relationships with suppliers' and 'consumer
options within the information industry.'"[41] Librarians often are
reluctant to provide ideas to private companies on needed information
services because these companies may make a profit on the sales of
products and services. The idea of profit in information is abhorrent
to traditionally trained librarians who see information as a freely
available idea, not as products and services to be sold in the
marketplace.

Companies developing home or office information and document
delivery services are in direct competition with libraries. Except for
specialized services aimed at specific groups, such as lawyers and
accountants, the target market for both libraries and private companies
is the middle and upper income, college educated consumer. This market
has both the necessary income and the motivation to provide viable
demand for home service.

Both libraries and private companies are crying "foul" because
they view the competitive situation as unfair. The information industry
claims it cannot compete on a price basis with services subsidized by
taxpayers. Libraries claim the information industry is invading their
sacred territory. By offering better quality and more convenient
service for a price, private companies are reducing the library's
market.

Is there a role for libraries in the world of electronics and
telecommunications? If so, what kinds of services should libraries
provide? If not, what will happen to libraries and who will serve the
poor, disabled, and disadvantaged who must rely on subsidized service?
It has been noted that "service to the public could be provided without
the library building, without buying books, without cataloging, without
circulation, without most of the trappings now associated with the
library institution."[42] This service would rely on well-trained information specialists with access to a variety of data bases and sources.
The scheme would be based on librarianship's evolving into a
concept of problem solving and away from the idea of document
preservation.

It is likely that some libraries will continue to exist as book
and document distribution centers. Taxpayers' support will depend on
public and social policy resolutions. If current library users can
purchase services through the private sector, will taxpayers be willing
to subsidize book collections in case someone who cannot pay wants to
use them? The current economic and political trends indicate that taxpayers will give up library service when it is in competition with fire,
police, and other services; however, taxpayers may be willing to
subsidize individuals who need or want to use the library.

Some public libraries may find a raison d'etre in children's services, especially in areas where school libraries are weak or open only
during school hours. Communities interested in preschool programs are
likely to retain children's libraries.

Other libraries will choose to integrate technology into their
operations even if it means buying services from the private sector and

charging fees. Libraries involved in computer-based services and interactive television services will find ways in which the library can enhance and complement these services.

There is also a possibility that some libraries will cease to exist. When publishing and information distribution cease to be paper dependent, there may be no need for libraries in some communities.

Academic and school libraries have better chances of survival because they are part of the formal education system. Academic libraries, however, may change dramatically. As higher education enrollment declines, funds will get tighter while competition among faculty members for research grants, promotions, and tenure will increase. Faculty will access information banks from computer terminals in their homes and offices. The academic library may function primarily in the areas of document delivery and/or preservation. Libraries in research institutions may provide more tailored information services to meet the needs of faculty researchers.

The school library or media center will undergo the least amount of change in terms of its purposes and objectives. It will offer a diversity of electronic and audiovisual material for students and teachers. School libraries with computer-based systems could become the locus of initial instruction in information finding especially in secondary schools.

## Conclusions

The amount of tax money available for libraries will decline in the next ten years. This decline will be brought about by reduced rates of government spending, continuing inflation, competition among public services, the aging of the population, and the public desire for greater amounts of discretionary income. During the same ten-year period information production and dissemination will be revolutionized by cheaper computers and telecommunications. The energy crisis will preclude unnecessary travel, especially short automobile trips. Electronic mail and message systems will be widely available. By the mid-1980s people will be able to access a variety of information banks from their homes and offices. Many traditional library services will be made obsolete by these developments.

The future of the library as we know it is in doubt. Many libraries will adopt the new technology and create complementary and supplementary services. Some libraries may provide services only to special groups, such as small business, children, and professional groups. Municipalities will encounter increasing difficulty in freely supporting public library services. Policy makers are likely to seek a compromise position between fully subsidized library service and fee for service. A minimal level of service could be provided with tax funds while fees support special or expedited services.

Librarians need to be aware of the social, economic, political, and technological environments within which they work and be prepared to adapt their professional lives to society as it is. The problems and the unpleasant trends will not go away, but the profession can turn these problems into opportunities and create a richer life for themselves and the people they serve.

## References

1. Forecasting International Ltd., Potential Impacts of Automation and User Fees Upon Technical Libraries, for the National Science Foundation (Springfield, VA:  National Technical Information Service), p. 97.  (PB 271418).

2. Elizabeth Stone, American Library Development 1600-1899 (New York: Wilson, 1977), p. viii.

2. Jesse H. Shera, Foundations of the Public Library Movement in New England 1629-1855, (Chicago:  University of Chicago, 1949).

4. Stone, American Library Development, p. 155.

5. Lawrence J. White, The Dilemmas of the Public Library (New York: New York University.  Faculty of Business Administration, 1978), p. 7.  (Working Paper Series #78-86).

6. Richard De Gennaro, "Pay Libraries and User Charges," Library Journal 100 (February 15, 1975):  366.

7. Ethel Crockett, UCLA Librarian 32 (June 1979):  47.

8. Fay Blake and Edith Perlmutter, "Libraries and the Market Place," Library Journal 99 (January 1, 1974):  p. 111

9. National Commission on Libraries and Information Science, Toward a Program for Library and Information Services:  Goals for Action an Overview (Washington, D.C.:  NCLIS 1978).

10. Don R. Swanson, "Libraries and The Growth of Knowledge," Library Quarterly 49 (January 1979):  21.

11. Thomas R. Buckman, "The Impact of Economic Change on Libraries," The Information Society:  Issues and Answers.  American Library Association's, Presidential Commission for the 1977 Detroit Annual Conference, (Phoenix, AZ:  Oryx Press, 1978), p. 49.

12. Zoia Horn, "Charging for Computer-Based Reference Services:  Some Issues of Intellectual Freedom," in Charging for Computer-Based Reference Services, edited by Peter G. Watson (Chicago:  American Library Association, 1978), p. 17.

13. Horn, "Charging for Computer-Based Reference Services," p. 17.

14. Paul A. Samuelson, Economics, 9th edition (New York:  McGraw Hill, 1973), p. 160.

15. Marilyn K. Gell, "User Fees 11:  The Library Response," Library Journal 104 (January 15, 1979):  171.

16. Cheryl A. Casper, "Subsidies for Library Services," Encyclopedia of Library and Information Science (New York: Dekker), (in preparation).

17. Gell, "User Fees 11," p. 171.

18. Indiana State Library. Statistics of Indiana Libraries (Indianapolis: the Library, 1976; 1977).

19. National Commission on Libraries and Information Science. Public Libraries: Who Should Pay the Bills. Washington, D.C.: NCLIS, 1978), p. 11.

20. The Wall Street Journal, October 24, 1979, p. 5.

21. The Wall Street Journal, p. 5.

22. Norman C. Saunders, "The U.S. Economy to 1990: Two Projections for Growth," Monthly Labor Review 101 (December 1978): p. 42.

23. Arthur Andreasseu, "Changing Patterns of Demand: BLS Projections to 1990," Monthly Labor Review 101 (December 1978): 54

24. Michael E. Levy, "Shedding the 'Free Lunch' Syndrome: A New Federal Budget Policy," Business Economics 15 (September 1979): 78.

25. Levy, "Shedding the 'Free Lunch' Syndrome," p. 84.

26. White, Dilemmas, p. 5-6.

27. American Library Association, A Perspective on Libraries (Chicago: ALA, 1979), p. 7.

28. White, Dilemmas, p. 6-7.

29. Chief Officers of State Library Agencies, The Role of Libraries in America (Frankfort, KY: the Officers, 1976), p. 20.

30. Chief Officers of State Library Agencies, Role of Libraries, p. 19.

31. Vincent E. Giuliano, "A Manifesto for Librarians," Library Journal 104 (September 15, 1979): 1839.

32. Ching-Chih Chen, et al., Citizen Information Seeking Patterns: A New England Study. Executive Summary Report for the White House Conference on Library and Information Services (Boston: Simmons College School of Library Science, 1979), p. 6.

33. Chief Officers of State Library Agencies, Role of Libraries, p. 19.

34. Ching-Chih Chen, Citizen, p. 7.

35. Phi Delta Kappa, A Decade of Gallup Polls of Attitudes Towards Education: 1969-1978, edited by Stanley M. Elain (Bloomington, IN: Phi Delta Kappa, 1978, p. 3.

36. Phi Delta Kappa, Decade, p. 121.

37. Phi Delta Kappa, Decade, p. 200.

38. American Library Association, Perspective, p. 11.

39. Harvey L. Poppel, "The Information Revolution: Winners and Losers," Harvard Business Review 56 (January-February 1978): 14.

40. Giuliano, "Manifesto," p. 1840.

41. Trevor Haywood, "The Librarian/Information Officer as a Consumer," ASLIB Proceedings 31 (September 1979): 435.

42. Giuliano, "Manifesto," p. 1840.

# THE ALLOCATION OF RESOURCES:
## AN ECONOMIST'S VIEW ON LIBRARIES

by

Richard L. Pfister
School of Business
Indiana University

Economists appear to be interjecting their views into many activities and fields outside their usually recognized areas of competence. They have been actively plying their trade in such diverse areas as medical care, health and safety regulation, environmental protection, energy, consumer protection, and so forth. They have also ventured into the analysis of libraries. Are economists simply arrogant in assuming theirs is the last word on almost any subject, or are there legitimate reasons for this widespread application of economic analysis?

These various institutions and activities all involve the use of scarce resources (labor, materials, equipment, buildings, land, etc.) to provide goods and services that benefit our society, and that is the subject matter of economics. To economists, the library is a productive unit that employs scarce resources to produce an array of educational, informational, recreational, and cultural services, and their interest is in evaluating the efficiency of resource use in all these activities. How much of society's resources should be devoted to producing these services? How should resources be allocated to achieve goals? Do present methods of determining resource use by the institutions result in efficient use of resources? Economists can and should play a role in answering these questions, whether they be raised concerning health care, business firms, energy, or library services.

Economists can establish standards for evaluating the efficiency of resource use and can suggest rules or guidelines to aid decision makers in promoting efficiency. The first general rule is that the benefits to society of any activity should exceed the costs of that activity. A comparison of the social benefits and the social costs is thus essential to prudent public policy with respect to the allocation of resources to any activity, including that of providing library services. A comparison of benefits and costs is also essential for the individual library determining the allocation of its limited resources so as to obtain maximum benefits for a community. Many problems arise in estimating benefits and costs. Later sections of this paper will deal with some of them. Because of such measurement problems, benefit-cost comparisons can only be a guide in helping make intelligent decisions and cannot be a substitute for judgment.

Economists are interested in more than whether benefits exceed costs; they also want to know the distribution of benefits and costs among various groups in a community. Do the methods of raising revenues

31

to finance library services take relatively more income from high, middle, or low income families? Similarly, do the benefits of the service accrue primarily to high, middle, or low income families? A particular service may yield benefits in excess of costs but be undesirable because of adverse effects upon the distribution of income.

In the private sector of our economy, we rely upon the forces of competition to ensure that resource use is efficient. Private markets yield prices that serve as signals to producers and consumers. Firms respond to these prices in deciding what to produce, how much to produce, and how to produce it. The lure of profits and the threat of losses cause firms to seek out efficient methods of production. The prices consumers are willing to pay serve as ballots in a continuous referendum to tell firms what to produce. Under ideal conditions, the resulting allocation of resources by the private market is efficient.

Economists recognize that private markets do not always achieve efficient allocation of resources. For most productive activities, private markets work well in serving social purposes. A major reason for the failure of private markets is the existence of important externalities or spillovers. Most analysts treat spillovers under the concept of collective or public goods. A collective good may exist for either of two reasons. First, the good may be such that when it is provided to one person, it becomes equally available to everyone--there is no way to prevent some from benefiting from the good or consuming it if it is provided at all. This characteristic is generally referred to as non-excludability. An example is air pollution abatement. If air quality in an area is improved, everyone in the area benefits and there is no way a business firm could sell air pollution abatement as a commodity. A market for such a good will not develop, because a firm could not charge for the good and therefore could not make a profit.

Second, if the good is provided to one person, it can be provided to others at no additional costs. This characteristic is generally referred to as non-exhaustibility. The consumption of such a good by one person does not reduce the amount available for others to consume. Air pollution abatement will again serve as an example. Either of these two characteristics of a good will either prevent the private sector from producing it or result in inadequate production.

Very few goods or services are pure collective goods in the sense that they meet one or both of these characteristics fully. But many goods and services are partly collective goods and partly private goods. A good that is partly collective because it is non-exhaustible may be produced privately but in smaller quantity than is socially optimal. A collective agency, usually the government, must intervene to achieve optimal resource use either by subsidizing the private producer or by producing the good itself. The next question I want to deal with is how libraries fit into this concept of a collective good.

## Library Services as Collective Goods

Even though we have some private libraries, we do not rely on private markets to provide the bulk of our library services. As a society we consider library services to be collective goods. What are the economic grounds for this decision? It would appear that libraries do not qualify as a collective good because of the non-excludability characteristic: it would easily be possible to exclude persons from using libraries unless they paid for the use. But library services could qualify as a collective good on grounds of non-excludability if spillover benefits are important; that is, if nonusers as well as users of library services receive benefits. Such spillovers are usually considered important for education, especially for primary and secondary education. User charges cannot be imposed on the beneficiaries of these spillovers; thus non-excludability would exist to the extent that spillover benefits exist.

Library services might also be considered collective goods if the marginal costs of providing services to additional users are declining and are very low. To have optimal resource use, marginal costs should equal marginal benefits, which are generally the prices paid by consumers. When marginal costs are below average costs, a private firm cannot charge a price equal to marginal costs and make a profit. Therefore, the private firm will charge a price equal to average costs (or higher) and will not supply the optimal amount--the price will be too high and the quantity too low. Governmental intervention will be necessary to achieve optimal resource allocation.

If a good is only partly a collective good and if exclusion is feasible, optimal resource allocation requires that a subsidy cover only part of the costs of the good. If, for instance, spillover benefits exist, the subsidy should cover only the value of the spillover benefits. Users should pay a fee equal to the private benefits realized by consuming the service. If providers of the service cannot cover total costs by charging a fee equal to marginal costs, the subsidy should cover just the shortfall, not total costs (assuming that total benefits exceed total costs). The main point is that subsidization of a partial collective good should not be 100% to achieve optimal resource use.

The next step is to see if any of these questions and issues can be resolved by existing data concerning library services. The available data on costs of library services are suggestive. A priori reasoning has led to the conclusion that the marginal costs of additional users of library services are very low--much below average costs and perhaps near zero. This reasoning would, of course, justify considering library services as collective goods. Empirical studies of library costs indicate that marginal costs of certain library services (book circulation in one case, journal circulation in another) are surprisingly high and surprisingly close to average costs. If these findings hold up, they greatly weaken the case for providing library services free to users.

Baumol has questioned whether any subsidy is justified if marginal costs are reasonably close to average costs and substantially greater than zero. A subsidy must be financed through taxes, and taxes have distorting effects upon the allocation of resources. Baumol concluded that a profit-making enterprise charging a price greater than marginal costs may actually be charging a price closer to the socially optimal one than that which would emerge under heavy but non-optimal public subsidy.[1] Before any firm conclusions are reached, however, we should await more and better cost studies.

Data on benefits are even less satisfactory than those on costs. Data on library usage permit some qualitative judgments to be made. Since I was previously involved in a study of public libraries, I will use some data pertaining to them to illustrate the approach. Each class of library and each service should be examined separately. The studies of usage of public libraries show that school-aged youths account for two-thirds to three-fourths of total usage. Obviously, much of the use by youths involves educational benefits, but some of it is recreational and does not involve significant social or spillover benefits. Most of the adult usage is for recreation and how-to-do-it information, both of which involve primarily private rather than social benefits. The key questions are how large are the educational benefits and what share of them are public rather than private? An upper limit on the value of the educational benefits for school-aged youths would be the cost to the public schools of providing comparable library services through the school libraries. To have a rational policy, we should consider whether the public or school libraries can provide these educational benefits at lower costs.

The Rand Corporation study of the public library of Beverly Hills made some rather crude estimates of private benefits of book circulation. The results are interesting but are only suggestive because of the crude methods used in developing the estimates. About half of the 42 classes of books had benefit-cost ratios greater than one. Mysteries, preschool fiction, and young adult fiction had the highest benefit-cost ratios. Among nonfiction books, those in art techniques, psychology, and business skills had the highest ratios.[2] The information in this study was developed primarily to guide the library in deciding on book purchases. Thus, it does not help much in deciding the broader question of how great spillover benefits are and how much subsidy might therefore be justified.

What does this discussion suggest concerning libraries as public goods? My conclusions are certainly tentative ones. Most of the available cost data show marginal costs for certain services to be below average costs though not much below. These services do not seem to qualify as collective goods on this basis. Spillover benefits of public libraries are undoubtedly significant, although many of the benefits are private. Ideally, the private beneficiaries should be charged for the private benefits. Obviously the "fine tuning" suggested by economic theory would not be practical, but it would seem practical to identify certain services as yielding predominantly private benefits and to impose user charges for them. Other services could probably be identified as yielding important spillover benefits and should be provided free.

## The Allocation of Resources within Libraries

Society will decide, through the political process, how much of its resources to devote to the public support of libraries. Library directors and staff may, of course, participate in that process and attempt to influence the amount of public support, but once that support is determined, each library will have a budget that limits the amount of resources it can have in providing library services. The library will then have to decide how much of each service it can produce and stay within its budget. This decision is similar to that of the profit-seeking enterprise, which has to decide what mix of outputs to produce and how to produce them. Both the business firm and the library need rules to guide them in making these internal allocations.

The private business, guided by market prices and by the quest for profits, has little trouble in making its allocation decisions. Competition and the threat of losses provide the incentive to seek the most efficient use of its resources. The library should presumably seek to allocate its resources to yield not maximum profits but maximum social benefits within the constraint of the budget. In the absence of charges for library services, what decision rules can the library use in the attempt to allocate its resources efficiently? Roland McKean has suggested that, in organizations not subject to the market discipline, decisions are the result of bargaining among different interest groups with different and perhaps conflicting objectives.[3]

Libraries are not highly visible organizations with respect to their internal decision making. Thus, the workings of the decision process are not obvious to those of us on the outside. I suspect that the library director makes most decisions after consulting with the staff and that these decisions are subject to the review of a board of directors. Thus, the allocation of the library budget is probably based upon the benefits of the various library services as perceived by the library director and staff. Library directors will presumably make allocation decisions they feel are the best, given their perceptions of the goals of the library.

The library profession, as with many professions, is not likely to agree that consumers know what is best for them or that services should be valued internally according to how much the public is willing to pay for them. Economists tend to defer to the judgment of consumers and to avoid telling them what they should want, valuing the benefits of any good or service according to the amount that the public is willing to pay for that good or service. To value services by what people should be willing to pay rather than by what they are willing to pay is to tread on dangerous grounds. What happens if professionals disagree on these subjective valuations? Or what happens if someone with widely different preferences gains control of the allocation decision? And what results if people simply refuse to use the services librarians believe they should use?

The advantage of relying upon evaluations by the public is that the outcome is not dependent upon subjective evaluations of any one individual or any professional group. If one does not agree with the public evaluations, he or she can work to change the public's values in the desired direction. But to ignore the public's preferences leads to a morass concerning the value of the services.

Regardless of what individual librarians say or what the professional associations say, I believe that individual libraries do give substantial weight to the preferences of the public concerning library services. Still, the library is not likely to estimate reliably the public's evaluation of the individual services in the absence of user charges. An expensive method of obtaining information about preferences would be to conduct a survey of actual and potential library users.

Respondents could be asked to value the individual services.  Without such a survey or without user charges, libraries probably respond mostly to the demands of the public as reflected in actual library usage.  This method does not yield information concerning marginal evaluations of each service, but it probably gets closer to the optimal allocation than would ignoring public preferences entirely.

Once a library has decided upon its goals or what mix of services it wants to provide, its interest should be to provide that mix in the most efficient manner, i.e., at the least possible cost.  To achieve efficiency in this sense requires analysis of cost-effectiveness of alternative methods of providing each service.  The library literature indicates considerable interest in cost-effective analysis.  Michael Buckland was really writing about cost-effectiveness in his article, "Toward an Economic Theory of the Library."[4]  But I disagree with his claim that we need a special economic theory of libraries.  What he was trying to do was simply to establish an objective function for libraries that did not involve profit maximization, but that is not a new theory.  There are various techniques in the economic theory of the firm for achieving a firm's goals efficiently, whether these goals involve profit maximizing or something else.  At the Indiana University School of Business, for example, we have a track in our MBA program for students who want to become managers in not-for-profit organizations.

If libraries were to have charges for all services, they could then readily determine the public's evaluation of the private benefits from these services.  Still, this information alone would not lead to optimal allocation decisions if there were spillover benefits for some services.  Efficient allocation might require user charges below actual costs for those services with spillover benefits.  The big advantage of user charges, however, is that they provide much useful information concerning the public's evaluation of services and thus provide an important guide to the library in allocating its resources internally.  In the absence of such charges, decision makers must rely much more upon subjective evaluations or judgments.

## An Overview of User Charges

When user charges are feasible, i.e., when the imposition of charges is relatively inexpensive and nonpayers can easily be excluded, they have three important advantages.  First, they can promote efficiency in resource allocation as has been argued previously in this paper.  With user charges, much better estimates can be made of the benefits of library services.  With better estimates of benefits, society can allocate resources to achieve greater social benefits and individual libraries can use their own resources more efficiently.  Second, charges force users of library services to pay for the private benefits they realize, so that services will not result from the redistribution of income--the apparent incidence of public library benefits and costs suggests that these libraries redistribute income from lower to higher income groups.  Third, user charges yield revenue that might permit library services to remain at existing levels or even increase when local government budgets are tight.

The recent discussion of user charges in the library literature

appears to have been the result of information storage and retrieval
with computers, especially with respect to data bases and bibliographies. Private companies have developed computer based services for
sale. Libraries are now faced with the problem of whether to subscribe
to such services, and if they do, whether to pass the costs on to users
of the services. To me as an economist, this situation would seem to
be ideal for a user charge. If this new service is one for which there
is sufficient demand, libraries could provide it as an additional service without cutting back on other services. Resources devoted to the
service would be used efficiently in the sense that they would provide
benefits at least equal to or greater than costs. Without user
charges, libraries would not be able to provide this service to their
users without diverting resources from other services since increased
budgets seem unlikely.

Some economists oppose user charges in specific instances on the
grounds of equity. User charges may be regressive in that they take a
greater proportion of income from lower income groups than from higher
income groups. Those who take this position generally want to use a
subsidized service to redistribute income toward the poor. But user
data for public libraries show that low income groups use them very
little, and subsidized service appears to redistribute income from
lower to higher income groups. Nevertheless, the equity issue is a
relevant one for any discussion of user charges. The private market,
with its reliance upon prices, promotes efficiency, not equity. The
traditional view of most economists on this matter is that we should
use the price system to achieve efficiency and then use transfers to
achieve equity if we do not like the private-market income distribution.

Another potential objection to user charges is that they may be
administratively costly and difficult to impose. If they are costly
to administer, then it might be better to subsidize a service completely. The inefficiency of imposing the user charges might be
greater than that of foregoing them. In the case of library services,
however, the imposition of user charges for most services would seem
to be simple and inexpensive.

Some librarians vigorously resist any move toward user charges.
I want to examine some of these arguments in relation to the economic
analysis developed in this paper. Some librarians argue, as a matter
of principle, that the public has a "right" to have free library services. Librarians tend to be offended by the view that libraries are
businesses and should be run according to business principles. More
specific arguments against user charges have been made by Fay M. Blake
and Edith L. Perlmutter.[5] Their arguments are an attempt to refute the
economic arguments in favor of user charges.

Blake and Perlmutter disagree that user charges would lead to
increased productivity of libraries and state that the evidence really
does not exist to show that libraries have lagged in productivity
growth. They argue that output measures are lacking for library
services, so productivity cannot be measured. I agree that we do not
have satisfactory output measures that combine all library services
into one measure. This problem is common to most public services.
Actually, I would not argue that user charges would result in more
rapid productivity growth but that they would give rise to a one-shot

increase in social benefits per unit of input in producing library services. Increases in library productivity over time could occur simply as the result of constant attention to cost-effectiveness for whatever services are being produced. The output mix could be non-optimal but productivity increases could be as great as they would be if the same services were produced by private suppliers.

Blake and Perlmutter argue next that user charges for library services would not increase efficiency of resource use, because they would not take account of spillovers. I have pointed out earlier in this paper that the existence of spillover benefits or declining marginal costs does not require complete subsidy of the service but only subsidy for that share of the benefits or costs considered to be public. For many library services, it seems likely that the bulk of the benefits are private so that efficiency considerations call for user charges at least equal to marginal costs. For other services for which the educational benefits loom large and where the actual division between private and social benefits is not easy to estimate, the service could be provided free.

Another argument that Blake and Perlmutter rebut is that library users are "free riders" in that they use the library without paying even though they would be willing to pay for the use. The "free rider" problem is common to collective goods when user charges cannot be employed. Blake and Perlmutter argue that because of spillover bene-fits, libraries should not charge for services to get rid of the free rider. Their argument really comes down to the question again of how much of the value of the service consists of spillover benefits and how much consists of private benefits. If the benefits are primarily private, then user charges are appropriate and will force the former free rider to compare private benefits with the user charges.

The final argument concerns whether user charges would reduce the competition for public funds because of the revenue generated. Blake and Perlmutter assume that if the charges reduce the use of public funds by libraries, the most likely outcome would be a decrease in taxes and public spending. Resources would thus be shifted to the private sector from the public sector. They assume that competition for public resources would actually increase, apparently because advertising enables the private sector to get more of the consumers' dollars at the expense of collective goods. If this is their argument, then I disagree with it. There is no evidence to suggest that adver-tising by the private sector causes a greater total expenditure on private goods and a diminution of spending on public goods. In fact, the rapid growth in the share of GNP spent by the public sector in recent decades suggests the opposite.

The remainder of their paper consists of a criticism of the assumed efficiency of private markets. They suggest the public enterprises are or can be more efficient than private forms. I strongly disagree with their views on this issue. It is easy to find fault with the way our private market economy operates; it does have shortcomings. But most critics of the system compare the way it actually operates with the way another system would ideally operate. Although I am willing to debate this issue, I would not place it among the central issues that need discussing in connection with user charges for libraries.

In conclusion, I urge librarians not to recoil at the use of economic analysis in the study of libraries. Do not turn your backs on efforts to evaluate the benefits to society of library services. You cannot avoid evaluating these services either implicitly or explicitly. Whether you like it or not, any decision you make involves an implicit evaluation of these services. Why not participate in efforts to evaluate the services explicitly to provide better guidance to society and to libraries in making allocation decisions? Current developments in fiscal policies, such as sunset laws, zero-based budgeting, accountability requirements, and so on, suggest to me that the library profession must undertake serious efforts to justify economically the claims by libraries on our scarce resources or else see a continued erosion of the real resources devoted to producing library services.

## References

1.  William J. Baumol, et al, A Cost-Benefit Approach to Evaluation of Alternative Information Provision Procedures (Princeton, NJ: Mathematica, 1971).

2.  Joseph P. Newhouse and Arthur J. Alexander, An Economic Analysis of Public Library Services (Santa Monica, CA: The Rand Corporation, 1972). (R-848BH).

3.  Roland McKean, "The Unseen Hand in Government," American Economic Review 60 (June 1965): 496-506.

4.  Michael K. Buckland, "Toward An Economic Theory of the Library," in Economics of Information Dissemination: A Synposium (Syracuse, NY: Syracuse University, 1973).

5.  Fay M. Blake and Edith L. Perlmutter, "Libraries in the Marketplace," Library Journal 99 (January 1, 1974): 108-111.

OPPOSITION VIEWS

# WHAT'S A NICE LIBRARIAN LIKE YOU
# DOING BEHIND A CASH REGISTER?

by

Fay M. Blake
School of Library and Information Studies
University of California, Berkeley

In a 1978 issue of a library journal the editor, himself the
director of a large university library, expressed his irritation with
the debate now going on in the library world about charging direct user
fees. "The current arguments within the profession are becoming
tedious," he says. "The private sector is not going to offer its
services gratis, so if libraries wish to offer online services developed by the private companies they must either pass on the charges or
absorb them. This seems to be a straightforward, nondebatable issue.
Let's not waste more time on it."[1] I can hardly imagine how any more
non sequiturs could have been packed into three short sentences, but
it's the last one I want to deal with first: "Let's not waste any more
time on it." That kind of infantile impatience is not a singular phenomenon among librarians. We tend to skirt philosophical issues
because, of course, they are never as neat as technical problems and
because, utlimately, the solutions depend on effective political per-
suasion and action outside the safe walls of our own institutions. To
decide, out of hand, that it's a waste of time to consider the effects
of direct user charges in libraries, to decide, out of hand, that pass-
ing on or absorbing charges for on-line services is a nondebatable
issue, to decide, out of hand, that continuing arguments about this
issue are "tedious" and, therefore, undesirable is to guarantee that
direct user charges will become the norm, that a responsibility of
libraries toward our society will have been handed over to others for
resolution, or that we can all turn from wasting our time to concentration on such real issues as allocating materials budgets in institutions of higher education or devising a formula for estimating book
losses in an academic library--both the subjects of articles in the
same journal.

While I'm at it, let me just mention some of the anomalies in the
editorial. The private sector has never offered us anything gratis,
but we never argued that as a consequence we had a simple binary choice
between absorbing the costs for books or journal subscriptions or
directories or government documents or our own expensive catalogs and
charging users direct fees every time they wanted to use any of these
services. Why is this the only choice suddenly when we're talking

about on-line services? And why is it suddenly nondebatable? How we
have absorbed costs, whether we have passed on charges, to whom we pass
on charges, how we allocate our resources, and how we persuade the
whole society of its responsibility for funding have certainly always
been debatable and never straightforward. Why is it now and only when
we're considering on-line services? Or is there a hidden agenda, too?
Are we going to pass on in the form of direct user charges our costs
for books, which we also buy--and at hugely inflated prices--from the
private sector? We'd better keep on debating this issue, and we'd
better consider carefully what's "a waste of time."

Because there seem to be a number of misconceptions floating
around I'd like to state what I'm talking about when I oppose direct
user fees. First of all, I'm talking about publicly funded libraries,
that is, libraries--public, academic, research, whatever--the bulk of
whose funding comes out of the public till, taxes, taxes levied on all
of us, whether we use the library ourselves or not. Secondly, I'm
talking about the effects of charging such fees on the availability of
information. I am fully aware that all library services cost money and
that "there's no such thing as a free library." What I'm concerned
about is who pays, not whether we pay. There's a kind of irony worth
noticing in the fact that many libraries in the private sector do not
charge direct user fees. Two different kinds of special libraries in
California that I'm familiar with can be used as examples. The
Mechanics Institute, of which I'm a member, maintains San Francisco's
oldest library. I pay an annual membership fee that entitles me to
vote for the board of directors, to participate in meetings, and to
play chess at midnight in rather plush, Old World surroundings, as well
as to use the fine library. I do not pay each time I check out books,
consult the catalog, require reference services or pound the circulation
desk because some one else has just whisked away my favorite mystery.
At the Lockheed California library in Southern California, extensive
services are provided for the staff of Lockheed California and, through
interlibrary arrangements, for the users of many other special
libraries. Recently, all the company-generated technical reports were
fed into an on-line data base. Literature searches and bibliographies
as well as microfiche copies of the entire catalog of 25,000 citations
are available to onsite users of the library, to other units in the
company, and to other libraries of the corporation. The suggestion that
each user pay a fee for each on-line transaction would be hooted at.
Lockheed California provides this service to its users because, unlike
some publicly funded institutions, they recognize that ultimately
they'll reap the benefits of making information accessible.

You'd expect the spokespeople of the information industry to support the concept of user fees, primarily because the imposition of such
charges generally speeds up the purchase of on-line services. We've
even seen examples where, like drug pushers, the information hucksters
offer the initial services free, share costs for the next period and
then, once you've been hooked, lower the boom. Libraries, more often
than not, have not looked far enough ahead, have not planned sufficiently for the service, and have found themselves forced to institute user charges for the on-line service. But, as a matter of fact,
the private information industry is not insistent on the need for user

fees.  As long              damn where the
money comes f              ~ation
Industry Ass               1977
reversed hi               nat
libraries ·               ncy was
trying to               at it was
probably               irect user
fees.               c libraries,
in pub               caries should
becom               rs of direct user
fees               ciple of equal
acc               plement it?
               -term effects of
direct u.               ct is that we have
divided our u.               can and those who
can't pay.  This a.          osophical assumption:
that the richer a perso.         he or she is of information and the better use he      of that information.
Now, there is a school of social c     our country, the
so-called "neoconservatives," who claim  that.  Amitai Etzioni has
recently described their basic position:

> "Neoconservatives see inequality, at least certain forms of
> inequality, as a positive social feature.  They tend to see a
> society of equals as unwieldy and unworkable as an army composed
> only of foot soldiers.  Society may not require 'a ruling class'
> but it can no more do without its various elites--cultural,
> political, economic, social--than followers can do without
> leaders.  And, as long as inequality is based on talent and
> achievement, it is, according to neoconservatives, not only
> necessary but also quite fair."[2]

Talent and achievement are, of course, most easily measured by how rich
you are or have become.  Now, if that's the yardstick librarians are
using when they opt for user fees they're really exhibiting an unwar-
ranted arrogance.  What gives them the right to turn their backs on
another kind of basic assumption in American society:  the assumption
that everyone is entitled to access to education.  We set up free public
schools, paid for by taxes and not by user fees, and made them available not because everyone was going to end up equally educated but
because we don't know ahead of time who was going to benefit society
most as a result of education and certainly wealth is not a reliable
social indicator of who could take the best and fullest advantage of
education.
     Russell Shank, director of the UCLA Library and former president
of the American Library Association, warned in a speech at the
California Library Association Conference in December 1977 that the
recent institution of user fees, especially by federal libraries and
agencies, may be "a devastating attack on the fundamental philosophy of
public funding of the library to fill a social need.... We may be
experiencing a permanent shift in funding of social programs from a tax

on all for service to many, to a tariff to be paid by users for what
will be a service to few."[3]

And that's the second dangerous effect to direct user charges.
Not only does the fee deny full and equal access to information but it
begins to tailor design and planning to the needs of a few, the paying
few. No matter what your analysis of the needs of your whole community
may reveal, no matter how useful a service may be, no matter how effectively your library's resources can be organized to provide a service,
the ultimate test for development of services will not be the needs of
society but the ability and desire of a relatively few individual users
to pay for it. The ultimate effects of such constriction of services
can be devastating for society. Ultimately, the nature of the information itself can and will be changed. Look at the existing on-line
data bases as a foretaste. Overwhelmingly they provide bibliographical
access to information useful to business people, scientists, and tech-
nicians. You can find every last article on the marketing of square
tomatoes but most of the people in this country are not marketing anything but their labor; many of them can't afford to buy tomatoes, and
I don't see any signs of the development of an on-line national job and
job training data bank, because who'd pay for it? Certainly not the
unemployed who desperately need it.

In the early days of the debate on fees there were a number of
librarians who argued that when they were working with paying customers, they "really put out," and they worked harder at validating the
accuracy of the information they delivered. I note a conspicuous lack
of such an argument in recent reports, probably as a result of the huge
questions such comments raised about the social responsibility
librarians felt toward users who weren't shelling out at the transaction point. But the question still peeks shyly out from behind the
barrage of academic and research jargon. In a recent study, "The
Effect of User Fees on the Cost of On-Line Searching in Libraries,"
Cooper and DeWath found that when user fees were instituted librarians
spent less time at the terminal and more on the preparation of the
request, and that there was a sharp decrease in the time required to
process the requests for paying customers. "This reduction," say the
authors, "may be due to the integration of the DIALOG procedures into
the other library activities, a more experienced staff during the pay
period, as well as perhaps some pressure to provide prompt service to
paying users. The volume of requests was also much lower during the
pay period, which no doubt helped reduce backlog problems considerably."[4] Note these reasons: having reduced the number of users by
instituting direct user fees, librarians can proceed to give better
services to fewer and richer (and therefore more insistent because more
powerful) people.

So far I've dealt, more or less, with the almost immediate effects
of user fees. Librarians, even those who recognize the effects of user
fees on the collection and the distribution of information find themselves forced to impose charges because the services, especially the
manipulation of on-line data bases, are expensive while the library
budgets are shrinking or, at best, barely holding their own. Other
librarians claim that in a time of economic recession many other public
services take precedence over libraries. Miriam Drake of Purdue is

quoted in a report of a conference in Pittsburgh on The Online
Revolution in Libraries as  scoffing at those who oppose user fees for
placing "library service in the same category of public good as
national defense, the space program, government supported research,
and foreign policy.[5]  It may come as a shock, but I do put library
service in the same category of public good as the other sacred cows
Drake cites.  From the point of view of societal needs I would need
lots of convincing that our defense and space programs really are
greater public goods than library service and that it's a sensible
allocation of public resources to put $117.8 billion (24% of the total)
into defense and a mere $12 billion into our entire educational support
as the federal budget for fiscal year 1978/79 proposed.  Even if we
accept defense, space, research, and foreign policy as essential to the
public good, please remember that all of them rely heavily on information (or should), that the more informed the whole electorate is on
these subjects the wiser our decisions, and that information is what
libraries dispense.  I'm not even sure that library budgets have all
shrunk so drastically.  The big urban public libraries have been hit
hard, as have all services in our crumbling cities, but budgets in
such publicly funded libraries as the universities of California and
Texas are doing quite well, thank you, and probably could do even
better if we were doing our political homework.

All this brings me to some of the alternatives to direct user fees
that might be possible.  I'll use the California example because I'm
most familiar with it and most active in trying to implement some of it.
At the Palo Alto Institute I referred to earlier, the question of alternatives to user fees quickly became a hotly debated subject.  The
executive director of CLASS, California Library Authority for Systems
and Services, agreed to explore the possibilities of a pilot program
for the provision of access to on-line data bases through multiagency
funds from state, federal and municipal or county funds.  CLASS has
already established a service in which it serves as a broker for on-line
services and offers participating libraries substantial reductions in
fees.  Our unpredictable governor, Jerry Brown, made an appearance at a
California Library Association Conference expecting, and getting, kudos
for the successful passage of new, much improved funding legislation
for public libraries.  But that's not all he got.  A University of
California librarian brought to his attention the growing problem of
fees for services, got his quick acknowledgement that this sounded
elitist and undemocratic and his agreement to consider legislation for
alternatives.  Before the day was out a proposal was in the works for
the preparation of such legislation.  It's on its way.  An amendment to
the California Library Services Act is under consideration providing
for a state-owned on-line data base service that would provide to public
and academic libraries and to state agencies the most frequently used
data bases at a minimum charge.  The service would be available to state
supported agencies with a discretionary fund for librarians to use when
they judged a search necessary for a user who could not afford to pay.
Several California legislators have declared, sometimes in resignation
and sometimes in exasperation, that librarians dog their legislative
steps, that they do their homework and present both proposals and sup-
portive documentation, and library budgets show the results.  We need

not capitulate docilely to inequitable allocations of resources, and we
need not humbly assume that we're not very important in society.  This
being California, however, we have the other side of the picture, too!
It wouldn't be fair to leave you thinking everybody loves libraries.
In June 1979 the Jarvis-Gann initiative was padded and slashed some
$8 billion from property taxes.  Its effect on public libraries and
other public services has not been beneficient.  What Jarvis-Gann
should indicate to all of us is the need for rethinking how we pay for
public services and who pays how much?  If librarians don't contribute
significantly to the discussion, which will certainly be going on at an
accelerated rate everywhere, if we've already decided we'll only serve
those who pay at the door, we can look to the disappearance of some of
our institutions and we can look to a radically impoverished society.

For my final point, let me deal with a long-term proposal as an
alternative to user fees.  Our economy has moved significantly in the
last half century from manufacturing to services.  We have been able to
do so because our increased productivity enables us to produce goods
with less labor.  Services, then, absorb those who are no longer needed
in manufacturing process, and they must continue to be absorbed if we
are to avoid a deep recession.  Public services cannot continue to
develop unless we reallocate some of the resources of the country, and
what we need, therefore, is a federal tax on those industries that have
shown a greater than average rise in productivity rate, and a transfer
of that tax to the public institutions that provide information,
specifically libraries.  On the face of it, this may seem like the
punishment of the most efficient, but not really.  Increased productivity is essentially the result of the effective use of information,
especially the use of research and development information.  The Bureau
of Labor Statistics calculates that,

> "Technological innovation is . . . an important source of produc-
> tivity growth.  Much of this innovation is the result of organized
> research and development (R & D) programs; the amount, rate and
> location of spending on R & D gives some idea of the importance
> placed on this activity by both government and industry."[6]

Those industries that have increased their productivity rate above the
average ought to be persuaded to turn back a portion of their earnings
for two reasons:  1) their social responsibility to the society that
provided the research, education, and consequent information upon which
the increased productivity is based; 2) their enlightened self
interest, which should make clear that unless the public service
sector is increased, labor, displaced by increased productivity, will
be unemployed, unpaid, unable to buy what is being produced, and unable
to contribute sufficiently to the payment of taxes.  The tax on above
average productivity could, of course, not be confiscatory or so great
that it would become a disincentive, but a modest transfer of revenues
to the public information services would make far better economic sense
for all of us than hastily imposed individual user fees.  Let me end
with a quote from Wassily Leontiev, Nobel Prize winning professor of
economics at New York University:

"One way of meeting the threat of potential technological
unemployment is the creation of new jobs and the maintenance of
old ones through increased investment, in other words, through
economic growth.  But, this possibility has definite limits.
How fast would the economy, and with it the volume of investment,
have to grow in order to keep the number of long distance operators
from decreasing in face of the fact that each of them will soon be
able to handle ten million instead of a thousand telephone calls?
The rate of investment required to accomplish this end might turn
out to be so high that very little would be left for current consumption.  In the pursuit of full employment through a greater and
greater volume of productive investment the society ultimately
would find itself in the position of the proverbial miser who
deprives himself of the bare necessities of life while depositing
more and more in an already swelling savings account, and this
despite his steadily increasing annual income.  That is exactly
what might happen in the long run under the relentless pressure
of technological advance, if the forces of unrestricted cutthroat
competition were permitted--let's hope they will not be--to govern
the operation of the labor market and the conditions of
employment ...

"Thus, in the long run, the ability of large masses of the
population to benefit from technological advance will depend more
and more on the direct transfer of property income derived from
the ownership of capital and natural resources."[7]

## References

1.  "Editorial/User Fees," Journal of Academic Librarianship 3 (January,
    1978):  319.

2.  Amitai Etzioni, "The Neoconservatives," Partisan Review 44 (1977);
    431-32.

3.  Quoted in "Presidential Timbre," Library Journal 103 (March 1,
    1978):  520

4.  Michael D. Cooper and Nancy A. DeWath, "The Effect of User Fees on
    the Cost of On-Line Searching in Libraries," Journal of Library
    Automation (December 1977):  reprint.

5.  "The On-Line Revolution In Libraries," Library Journal 103 (February
    15, 1978):  440.

6.  "Factors Affecting Productivity Growth," in Productivity and the
    Economy (Washington, D.C.:  U. S. Department of Labor, Bureau of
    Labor Statistics, 1977, p. 61.  (Bulletin 1926).

7.  Wassily Leontiev, "Observations on Some Worldwide Economics Issues
    of the Coming Years," Challenge 21 (March/April 1978):  28-29.

# WHY SHOULD OUR USERS PAY TWICE?

by

Roger Stoakley
Deputy County Librarian
West Sussex, England

One of the gravest threats now facing the public library service
is the possibility of imposing charges on individual borrowers for the
loan of library materials.  At a time when the services traditionally
provided by local government are being reappraised in the light of
successive cuts in public expenditure it is not surprising that proposals have been made to charge for library facilities.  Such proposals
have been put forward by some for purely political advantage and by
others because of a genuine misunderstanding of the true concept of our
service.  It is likely that these people view the function of the
public library primarily to supply light reading.  They may also perhaps believe that libraries, being a public service, are tarred with
the brush of bureaucracy and are consequently overexpensive.  There is
every likelihood of their being joined by another group, irked by the
setbacks to PLR legislation, and who would welcome the ending of a free
library system.

Public libraries are the only source of recorded knowledge and
information freely available to all members of the community.  From
their inception they have been funded jointly by the community to pre-
serve their essential impartiality in serving the needs of all classes
of users.  If we are to have an educated and informed population we
need a strong and open library system.  If we believe in this basic
principle, one which librarians have striven to maintain for more than
a century and which has led to the development of one of the finest
public library systems in the world, then we are likely to have to
fight hard to retain it in the years ahead.

If we are to fight effectively we must be clear in our own minds
of the reasons why we object so strongly to a proposal that may appear
relatively innocuous to the majority of the public.  Our first and most
important consideration must be the principles at stake.  Our libraries
cater for the whole spectrum of public demand.  They have an additional
responsibility to provide the maximum freedom of individual choice from
resources which together represent all shades of opinion and relate to
every field of human experience and activity.  Free access to such
information is a vital pre-requisite of a democratic society and is

Reprinted with permission from Library Association Record 79 (April,
1977), p. 185-86.

available to the public at large only through the public library
system. Once charges are imposed not only are barriers erected but the
system becomes subject to pressures which are difficult to withstand.
We know that about 35% of the nation borrow from public libraries. The
proportion is larger if one includes those using the reference and
information facilities, the special services to schools, old people's
homes, the housebound and the handicapped. The appeal of our libraries
to pressure groups as a means of promoting their particular interests
regardless of their relevance in the community, is therefore considerable and librarians experience these pressures regularly. Our strength
in rebuffing attempts on our impartiality lies in the very fact that
our libraries are financed by the community to serve the needs of the
community and not those of individual subscribers who may well expect
the right to priority treatment, to restrict the choice of material to
that which they themselves may wish to see and to exclude items to
which they may take exception.

It has been argued in the past that charges might be confined to
the loan of popular material borrowed for entertainment rather than
serious study, or that charges should be imposed on all loanable
material, with students and old age pensioners exempted. But in each
case it is virtually impossible to know where to draw the line. Should
a child studying George Orwell or Jane Austen at school be subject to a
charge for borrowing "popular" material? Is it fair that the free
loan of serious reading material should be restricted to children of
school age and those students who can produce a current NUS card or
prove attendance at a recognized educational establishment?

The imposition of charges for the use of library facilities would
have an immediate and adverse effect both on library users and the
libraries themselves. The borrowers most likely to be discouraged
from using the service are those who probably have the greatest need--
young children, teenagers and those of little means. The degree to
which borrowers are discouraged is likely to relate to the size of the
charges imposed. Public libraries, in the absence of a more accurate
measurement of public use, have traditionally relied on issues and
membership figures as a means of justifying the allocation of increased
resources. The imposition of charges would inevitably lead to a substantial drop in the use of our services. A parallel effect can be
seen in the fall of reservations taken in those authorities which have
recently substantially increased their reservation fees. A drop in the
use of our services could only serve to accelerate the cuts already
imposed upon us.

The suggestion of a charge for the use of library materials is in
many respects illogical. The public library is not, of course, a free
service. It has to be paid for out of the rates and the rate support
grant in the same way as all other local authority services. If a
charge were imposed then by the same token dustmen should collect a fee
each time they empty the dustbin and firemen should collect a fee when a
disaster occurs at home. Our problem is that libraries convey neither
the sense of urgency nor necessity that characterizes other public
services such as fire and public health. The effect of libraries in the
community is long-term and subtle, yet equally important. The extreme
example of a householder deterred from calling the fire brigade to save

his blazing property because he could not afford the fee now seems ludicrous. But is it any less ludicrous to deter the potential library user in a society which is almost totally reliant on the ability of each individual not only to read but to draw upon its store of recorded knowledge simply because of the imposition of a fee he felt he could not afford?

On purely economic grounds there is little case for charging for library facilities. There are more than 10,000 public library service points in this country. They are used by people from all walks of life, every income bracket and virtually every age group. Within each community the contribution of our libraries to commerce, industry, education and cultural activities generally is extensive. It can be fairly said that libraries are one of the few local government services applicable to every sector of the community. The average cost of our public libraries is about £2.80 per head per annum. Compared with expenditure on education, roads and transportation, social services and the police, the cost of library services is minimal. Indeed the daily cost of public library services to the ratepayer is less than the price of a national daily newspaper. On these grounds it can be reasonably argued that public libraries represent the best value of almost any local government service.

Quite apart from discouraging the use of the service there is unlikely to be much, if any, financial gain for libraries if charges were introduced. The income would probably be small in terms of annual library budgets, which in many authorities now stand at over two million pounds. Then again there is no guarantee that the charges collected by libraries would be used to enhance or even offset the cost of running the service. It would indeed be ironic if unscrupulous authorities used this additional source of income to help finance their other more costly services. More importantly, if we were to have the principle of charges imposed upon us, it might not be long before we were required to be self-supporting. This would lead rapidly to the demise of amenity services and encourage concentration on popular reading, bringing in a good return at the expense of the more worthwhile material and services that characterize the public library service of today.

There can be no doubt that public librarians would be well advised to appraise both their staff and their local authority members of the harm that could accrue, not only to our library system but also to our society, if the concept of a free service were in any way weakened.

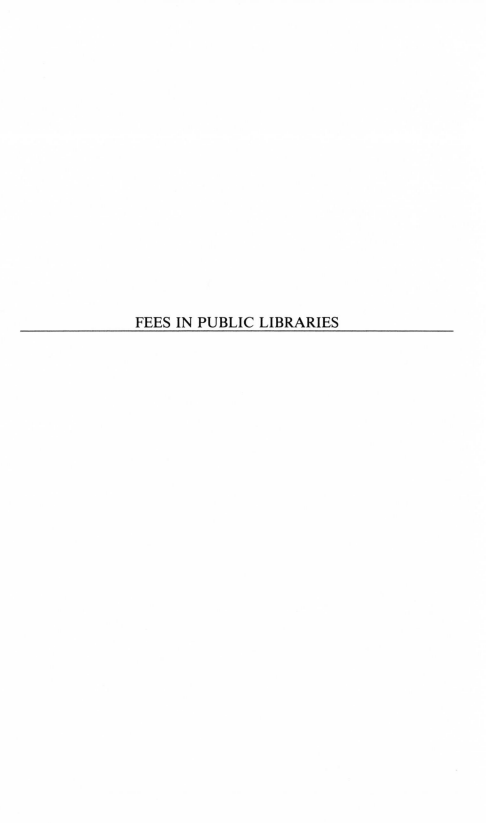

FEES IN PUBLIC LIBRARIES

# INFORM:
# AN EVALUATION STUDY

by

Grieg Aspnes

[The original Editor's Note that accompanied this article read as follows: "The following is the author's report to the Board of Directors of INFORM, an experimental consortium of libraries to the Minneapolis-St. Paul metropolitan area designed to provide "in-depth" reference service to clients for a fee. The participating libraries are: the J. J. Hill Reference Library, the Minneapolis Public Library and the University of Minnesota Libraries. The Office of Public Libraries and Interlibrary Cooperation participates on the governing board as a result of having provided the initial funding through a grant from state aid for interlibrary cooperation."]

## Introduction

"Why was Roger Bacon called the 'father of science'?"

"He was in the monastery; they were writing a new encyclopedia. The question was the number of teeth in a horse's mouth; a bitter debate went on for several days, and there were three theories--32, 34 and 37. Everybody had firm documentation for his position.

"Some went back to St. Augustine, some to various papal encyclicals, Roger Bacon, not a particularly energetic person and somewhat of a dreamer, was looking out the window, and he saw a horse, and had the temerity to suggest that they go count the number of teeth in the horse's mouth."[1]

Although this report is called an "evaluation study" it is basically an attempt to learn if there is an adequate market for INFORM--an information service on a fee basis. The obvious solution is to look the horse in the mouth--to go out and count the customers and examine their attitudes toward INFORM, and also try to learn something from non-users.

This is not scholarly research. There are too many variables, too many unknowns, too many elements of prediction and extrapolation, and the subject is too complex and subjective to be quantified to any great degree.

Reprinted with permission of Office of Public Libraries and Interlibrary Cooperation, Minnesota Department of Education, from Minnesota Libraries 24 (Autumn 1974), p. 171-85.

Nevertheless, it is a serious attempt at determining the value and viability of INFORM.

To make this report meaningful, it will not evaluate photocopy service. Photocopy service--for a fee--has been available from the J. J. Hill Reference Library (for one) for at least the past 20 years.

This study will concern itself with "INFORM" as a distinctive type of information service provided by public and academic libraries on a fee basis. It will try to answer the following main questions:

Is INFORM needed?
Is INFORM successful?
Is INFORM a justifiable activity?
How should INFORM be financed?
Does INFORM have a future?

The answers found in this report are based on:

1) Interviews with the members of the INFORM working committee.

2) Interviews with users and nonusers of INFORM.

3) Interviews with Special Librarians (mainly in business and industry).

4) Literature on the subject.

5) A survey of similar other services throughout the U.S.

6) My 30 years' experience as a special librarian serving industry in the Twin Cities, and a regular user of all the libraries involved.

The answers can be summed up as follows:

1) INFORM offers a service very much needed by our society, by business and industry, and by individuals, as information becomes more and more important to our daily lives and more and more difficult to organize, to find, and to use.

2) INFORM has been successful--to varying degrees and in varying ways, with various individuals, depending on a wide variety of circumstances. But it still has a long way to go to reach its stated and advertised objectives.

3) INFORM is a justifiable activity. It performs an important and valuable service that is not conveniently and efficiently available through any other means.

4) INFORM should try to pay for itself. This also offers the challenge of trying to measure and justify the value of information services.

5) INFORM has a great future. It should continue and be expanded. It can become an important part of the public and academic libraries' service to society. And it offers rich opportunities for them to explore, to test and to answer some critical questions about information service--their responsibilities and the best ways and means for providing it.

## Is INFORM Needed?

"The purpose of INFORM is to offer, on a fee basis, an

information service to anyone contracting for the service. The objective of INFORM is to provide the user with access to library resources and professional skills to a degree not available through ordinary reference service."

> --from the Preamble to the original
> agreement among the 4 participating
> libraries, 1/5/72

There can be little doubt that this type of information service is very much needed. In the past 20 years a great number of special libraries and information centers have been organized and are supported by business and industry, governmental agencies, trade and professional associations, research institutes and other for-profit and nonprofit organizations. They represent an awareness of two important facts of life:

1) That information is a valuable, necessary commodity and resource; that they who are not willing (or able) to learn from the mistakes and progress of history are doomed to re-invent the wheel; and

2) That there is far more information available and constantly being produced than any individual or group can possibly control without qualified, professional help.

Peter Drucker has summed it up:

"Knowledge, during the last few decades, has become the central capital, the cost center, and the crucial resource of the economy. New knowledge, rather than capital or labor, now produces productivity. . . . The impact of cheap, reliable, fast and universally available information will easily be as great as was the impact of electricity."[2]

This is not a unique observation. "Knowledge, rather than science, has become the foundation of the modern economy. Like electricity or money, knowledge is a form of energy that exists only when it is doing work" (Buckminster Fuller).

"The modern corporation should put a new branch on its VIP tree-- vice president for information" (Journal of Commerce).

And in a recent issue of the Congressional Record (May 9, 1974, p. S 7539): "All of us are acutely aware that without access to information and analysis of the highest quality--readily available and in a form which we can use--Congress cannot hope to fulfill its constitutional responsibilities. . . ."

Enough has been written about the great growth of literature in all subject fields to make an "information explosion" all of its own. The proliferation--in recent years--of services similar to INFORM, provide more proof. Perhaps the oldest and best known is S.V.P., a private French company which has been operating since 1935. Its 15,000 clients are almost all business firms who find in S.V.P. a source that can provide information more quickly, more cheaply, more comprehensively than the companies can do it for themselves. Nearly all questions (average: 4,500 per day) concern business operations, taxes or law, protocol, sources of supply.

S.V.P. will also book and deliver travel tickets, reserve theater seats and hotel rooms, provide translations, renew passports, lend TV sets and provide temporary office help.

S.V.P. has built up such a solid backlog of services rendered that it is almost second nature for French businessmen to dial its phone number whenever they need a question answered quickly.

The John Crerar Library in Chicago is the best illustration in the U.S. of information service on a fee basis (limited to paid-up members and the fields of science and technology). In recent years, a number of private organizations have tried to answer this need for speedy, convenient, accurate information service.

Some of them include:

Ayer Information Center (Philadelphia)

FIND (New York City)

Information Unlimited (Berkeley, Calif.)

INTERFILE (World Trade Center, NYC)

The Information Source (founded 1961 as Advertising and Marketing Research Library, Los Angeles)

Information Clearing House (New York--based affiliate of S.V.P.)

The Center for International Business (formerly part of World Trade Center, now part of Pepperdine College, in San Francisco and Los Angeles)

Information Resources (Toronto, Canada)

Warner-Eddison Associates (Lexington, Mass.)

Library Reports & Research Services, Inc. (Westminster, Colo.)

Technical Transfer Service (Chicago, Ill.)

Information for Business (New York)

In some states, college libraries have tried to provide this type of information service. Some examples:

The Information Exchange Center (Georgia Institute of Technology)

Industrial Information Services (Southern Methodist University)

Information for Industry (North Carolina State University)

Regional Information & Communication Exchange (Rice University, Houston)

There are, no doubt, many others, both public and private. One report claims "Two dozen, at least" and James Dodd of Georgia Tech says he has visited about 20 information centers similar to his.[3]

The very fact that so many such services exist seem to argue that there is a strong need for a service that provides information quickly, accurately, on any subject, completely, but packaged to fit the customer's specific needs. But for INFORM the answer must be sought closer to home. The INFORM customers that I talked with generally agreed on the value of this service. The response of one (a small chemicals manufacturer) was typical:

"INFORM is definitely worthwhile. I have tried to find some of this information for myself, but digging into those reference books and finding where the material might be is a study in itself, and they certainly can get through them a lot faster than I could. I sure would turn to them again, if I felt the need for something similar."

And a research organization said:

"This is a viable service.  More people should be using it.
I have encouraged others in our firm to use INFORM.  It is a good
substitute for having our own librarian, which we are not able to
justify.  We look on it as a sub-contractor for information, just
as we do for commercial design, packaging, etc.  Simpler, cheaper,
more efficient than trying to do it ourselves."

Most of the other responses were positive and encouraging.

"Firms outside the Twin Cities should be able to use INFORM
too."

"I hope INFORM will be continued."

"More people should know about it.  Any firm would gain by
having INFORM do searching for their information."

"Is there a need for this service?  Absolutely!"

"It is a viable service.  People should use it more."

"I have encouraged other people in our firm to use INFORM.
There are a lot of good prospective customers out there who could
make good use of INFORM."

"If you told me they were going to stop INFORM, I would be
mad.  That's how strongly I feel about it."

"I hope they will keep expanding as the demand increases,
so they will always be available."

"Anything I can do to help keep them alive, I'll be glad to
do it.  That's the best testimonial I can offer."

"If I had had this kind of library service when I was in the
consulting business, I could take their $20/hour and sell the
service for many hundreds of dollars as a consultant."

"We are not really making the use of INFORM that we should
be."

"INFORM is the kind of information service that is hard to
come by."

"I should think the whole community could use INFORM and that
it will keep going."

"I hope INFORM continues.  We don't use it a lot, but when we
do, we really need it.  If service like this is not available
easily elsewhere, then I would have to rate INFORM as very
important."

One swallow does not make a summer.  Nor do interviews with 20
satisfied customers make a market survey.  On the other hand, cold
typed words on paper cannot convey the sounds of enthusiasm and
encouragement that were attached to those words.  The final proof of
the pudding, of course, has to be the repeating.  How many customers
will come back for more of the same, and willingly pay for the privi-
lege?  How many will act as salesmen for INFORM and bring other customers with them?  We have only a small glimmer of this so far, a
straw in the wind, but it is encouraging.

Number of hours searching time for INFORM

Minneapolis Public Library

| | |
|---|---|
| 1971 | 235 hours |
| 1972 | 500 hours--up 115% |
| 1973 | 763 hours--up 53% |

If 1974 shows a similar growth, would that not be convincing
proof that INFORM's services are needed, recognized and bought?
    You will note differing statements about "who needs INFORM most."
Some say "the large organization, whose problems are large and complex
and can justify paying for such service."  Others claim "the smaller
firm that cannot afford to have its own information service or
resource."  Both are right.  And so are Drucker, Fuller, et al.  Information is a necessary resource, as tangible and as valuable (in many
ways) as land, buildings, equipment, capital, credit, personnel.  Information is meat and bread for the researcher; it is also vital to
decisionmaking in all fields, on all levels; the right information at
the right time to the right person(s) in the right form, can make great
improvement in the creative effort, in discovery and development of new
ideas, new products, processes, procedures, techniques.
    A PERSONAL NOTE:  For the past 18 years I have acted as co-chairman
(with Audrey Grosch) of the Special Libraries Association's Consultation
Committee in Minnesota.  In that 18 years, we have been asked for help
by some 150 different organizations.  They included business and professional firms, local, state and federal governmental agencies,
research institutes and non-profit organizations.  Each was convinced
they had an "information problem" and needed help in deciding what to
do about it, how to solve or ease the problem.  Of that 150, 30 now
have full-fledged special libraries, manned by professional personnel.
The others, each for their own reasons, made other decisions.  Some
learned how to solve their problem by other means; some decided to
postpone action or felt the problem was not important enough to justify
further attention or expense.
    In each case, however, the pattern was much the same.  The elements
of need were there:

        "We have small collections of books, etc. all over the place,
    but nobody knows where anything is when we want to find it."

        "We waste too much time looking for information."

"Our collection is a mess; it should be organized better."

"We need a better system for getting information for market studies (or technical research, or planning programs, etc.)"

This is only the tiny tip of a great iceberg.  The value of information service (like the value of insurance) has to be in the eye of the beholder.  To paraphrase a popular advertising slogan, "EveryBODY needs Information."  Not everybody realizes it, however.  We will discuss what to do about that in the section of this report titled "FUTURE."

So the answer to our first question "Is INFORM needed?" has to be a positive and determined "Yes."

## Is INFORM Successful?

The answer depends (as it so often depends) on how you define the question.  The answer has to be a qualified "In some ways,'Yes'; in some ways, 'No'."

Has INFORM succeeded in achieving its stated objective:  "To provide . . . access to library resources and professional skills . . ."?  For the small groups who have used INFORM, Yes.  But for the great number of non-users, No.  We can only guess how many non-users, but note in the comments of the customers the frequent comment that:

"Most downtown law firms should eventually make use of INFORM."

"INFORM could be of service to customers in Rochester, southern Minnesota, western Wisconsin, etc."

"Most businessmen do not know about INFORM, don't realize what they can do.  A lot of them would be elated to find such a service is available."

"We don't use them as much as we could . . ."

"I should think the whole community could use INFORM."

"Other patent attorneys should be able to use it and don't realize it exists."

"If it were better known, you'd probably find a lot of smaller firms using it."

Certainly, INFORM has not succeeded with the special librarians of Minnesota.  The basic problem was summed up best by the executive of one large industrial firm who supervises his company's various libraries:

"We haven't really made the full use that I think should be made of the INFORM service.  I have tried to encourage our librarians, when they are loaded to the gills with work--and it is a non-proprietary matter--that (INFORM) is a good backstop.  But there is this feeling 'I'd rather do it myself' and it is hard to get them out of this rut.  For years we wondered how we could get our hands on the millions of sources at the U of M--now we have a handle on it and we are not really making the use of it that we should."

Why don't people use INFORM, or why do they use it once but not return?  The answers to this vital question are beyond the scope of this study, aside from the implications that appear in the information we did gather.  Some of these implications--so far as librarians are concerned--seem quite obvious!

"We don't use it here; most of our information is highly technical."

"We feel ourselves capable of doing just about anything and more than they can do.  Also, we feel the expense is considerable. If our library staff was ever cut down, I imagine out of desperation it might be necessary [to use INFORM]."

"INFORM is a good idea, but their librarian is so overloaded with inadequate staff . . . if she could get some help, she could do much more than she is doing now."

"Most of our questions are 'do it today' or the next couple of days.  And we are close enough so it is easy for us to run down there and do our own searching."

"I didn't know that you could call the U of M and they would send you books."

"I have an assistant; I send her down to the library because it is cheaper.  My budget is not that big that I can afford INFORM. I couldn't justify a 2 hour search."  (This librarian is 10 miles from the nearest INFORM source.)

"The big firm that has its own librarian shouldn't have to use it."

"Maybe it is my ego, but I haven't had any trouble finding the stuff my people need.  No one can really do it the way I can do it."

"We are pretty well self-contained in our field.  It should be very useful to a small company without its own library.  Can you borrow materials through INFORM?  I didn't realize that. Thought it was just $18/hour for searching."

"It seems that I have been able to take care of the questions without going anywhere else, except when I call other special

librarians.  I always have them to fall back on.  Maybe it is a
cost thing."

"I have never used it because it is convenient for me to stop
by the library.  I can quickly find the stuff myself.  We pay only
$6/hour for the same kind of service from the World Trade Center
in San Francisco."

"Management seems to feel that $18/hour is too much money."

Such comments are startling when they come from professional
librarians.  They represent some strange misconceptions and fallacies
about library service, what it is, what it is supposed to be and about
the value of information.  INFORM cannot be blamed for these misconceptions; but INFORM also cannot claim complete success so long as
many of its prime prospects do not understand their own or INFORM's
part in this important enterprise.
How much IS information worth?
How do you measure the value of information service?
How do you measure the efficiency of any library or librarian, of
any index or other means for locating and providing information?
On what basis does a librarian--or an organization--decide if it
is "cheaper" for the librarian to travel to the library and do his own
searching rather than have INFORM do it for $18/hour?  A true cost
analysis would have to include:
The cost of the librarian's time, from the moment he leaves his
desk until he returns.  Plus the costs of transportation, parking, etc.
Plus the cost to his organization of his not being at his desk, able to
meet and serve customers (in person or by phone), plus the value of
what he might do during the time when he is driving, parking or
otherwise not actually doing the professional searching in the outside library.
Finally, it would be helpful to know just how efficient any
librarian is, searching in a strange library compared with a librarian
who works in that library every day.
These are not the only important factors, of course, but if
special librarians were more cost and efficiency-conscious, they might
be more critical of the ideas "We can do it better" or "It didn't cost
much because we did it ourselves."  Neither should be believed without
careful examination.  This provides one of INFORM's great opportunities;
to convince us special librarians that INFORM can help us be more efficient, can help us do our jobs better, more efficiently, more quickly.
Most of us recognize the need to pay heavy sums for CHEMICAL ABSTRACTS,
or ENGINEERING INDEX, the Encyclopedia Britannica or the reports of the
Research Institute of America.  As one special librarian saw it:

"None of us could survive (as librarians) without using other
resources.  It has been my experience that any time you provide a
useful service, you have bitten off more than you can chew.  And
if you use something to back up that service, it doesn't decrease
the service, it just increases.  The more you give people something

that is good, the more they will want.  INFORM is no different from having data bases on-line or like calling another special library."

If you define INFORM's objective to "provide access to library resources . . ." success has been achieved.  Access has been provided. And a small number of individuals have used the service.

But if "Success" means more--if it means something like providing the service to everyone who can make good use of it--then INFORM still has a long way to go.  The conscientious special librarian uses his spare time to wonder how many people in his organization do not use his services who could have, should have and if they had, would have done their jobs better.  In business it is called "the untapped market," INFORM has hardly begun to tap its market.

Those who have used INFORM generally agree that it has been suc-cessful, i.e., their requests for information were answered promptly, completely, specifically.  When asked on what basis they judged the accuracy and reliability of the information provided to them, their answers were very interesting:

"The last time, one of our secretaries tried to find the information and couldn't find it, INFORM found it for us within two days."

"We never really know for sure that the information is all that we need, but we have never felt let down.  We seemed to be satisfied with the results, they seemed to have done a thorough job."

"Their replies have been very adequate; even if a bit more than I need, it is helpful.  I can always wade through it."

"I often already have information on the subject from various sources compiled before going to INFORM.  So I will know that what INFORM gives me is factual; sometimes they will give me what I already have, but more which I did not have."

"Usually we have done some research before, and we can see what they have given us and how it compares with what we have done."

"On the strength of their research I put together a 30 page recommendation and report that . . . enabled us to move into the field without having any previous experience in the business.  I have never asked them for anything that they haven't come up with something that expanded my knowledge quite a bit."

"Our searching has to be done in the U.S. Patent Office, and there you are limited to things that have been patented.  But when you want to go beyond that, we have found INFORM to be a good, reliable, reasonable cost way to go."

"I got out of it what I was looking for."

"The information they have provided is good, judged by my own experience in the subject.  I have hunted through libraries.  I have considerable acquaintance with what I am looking for, and based on that, I would say they have done very well."

So we can sum up:  INFORM has had some success.  Most of its customers are satisfied with the service; some came back for more, some recommended the service to others, most think INFORM is a good idea.

But "success" has many sides.  Cost is one.  Was this success worth what it cost; how much will future successes cost?  Priorities is another aspect.  How important is success in this venture compared with the library's other responsibilities?  Are they related or interdependent in any way?  Does success in one endanger success in any of the others?

INFORM's success to date is very minimal if judged against its stated objectives and against the vast potential need for this kind of specialized information service:  When one INFORM library reports that of 8,000 queries per year from business and industry, 95% are for photocopy service and only 25 queries "are truly INFORM type;" when another library says they have not had 10 INFORM-type customers since their program began; and a third shows only 10 INFORM-type questions handled during 1973.

## Is INFORM A Justifiable Activity?

The stated purpose and objectives of INFORM imply a commitment to an information service virtually without limit.  The past two years have brought some tests of that commitment, with requests that went far beyond the usual public or college library experience.  Some required many weeks of intense work, others involved searching far beyond the resources of the individual library, including long-distance phone calls and interviews that sought information not available via conventional media.

Much of the data had to be sifted, filtered, evaluated and packaged to make it helpful to the customer.  Rigorous deadlines had to be met.

These examples typify the ideal of special librarianship which John Cotton Dana a long time ago termed "Putting Knowledge to Work."

A sharper definition has come from Herbert White, former IBM and NASA librarian, past president of both the Special Libraries Association and the American Society for Information Science.

"The Special Library is that type of library which puts the needs of the user and the service requirements of meeting those needs above the principle of maintaining library service in accordance with any particular established traditions and techniques.  Further, this service must be performed on the terms needed by the user, whether or not they conform to the library's own traditional pattern of operation."[4]

What reasons does a tax or foundation-supported agency have for trying to provide such a service on a fee basis?

We have seen evidence (part one this report) that a specialized information service is greatly needed and is appreciated by those who receive it. We also know that very few charters for "public" libraries include responsibility for such a service. Every library has to define its limits of responsibility. In a private organization, these can be as broad and as deep as the organization is willing to pay for.

But the limits for "public" libraries have both a traditional and practical basis. One viewpoint:

> "The public library has a long term objective to satisfy the cultural needs of the people in the community while the private research or technical library has to dispense a more tangible product on a day-to-day basis. The public library, for example, can legitimately classify as unreasonable an urgent request for specific information in a conveniently wrapped package. On the other hand, for the research organization or private industry, responding to such a request can save time and money and thereby make the request reasonable."[5]

This boils down the issue to some simple questions, "Should a "public" library try to provide this no-limits type of information service? Does it have a priority among the library's basic responsibilities? If it is to be done, how is it to be paid for?"

Many special libraries in business and industry have been abolished, or abandoned to the care of a clerk or secretary in order to "save on expenses." The real reason is that management does not see proper value received for the dollars expended. This makes most special librarians acutely aware of their responsibility constantly to justify their place in the company budget.

Public and academic libraries are seldom cancelled. But they may suffer a slow, painful financial attrition at the hands of the community or the academic administration. The results and the reasons are much the same. For academic libraries, "the bottomless pit" is a cliche with grim overtones.

> "Only the librarian (of all college administrators) is unable to place any limits on his needs."

> "The long-held article of faith that the library is a Good Thing and somehow self-justifying is questioned."

> "Nobody yet appears to have the slightest idea how to make a cost-benefit analysis of the contribution of the library."[6]

The public library suffers from a similar malady. Studies indicate that only a very small part of the general public makes intensive use of their libraries. And Goddard argues that 75% of all public library circulation is accounted for by school children.[7] This makes it easy to ask: How can society justify so much money for the benefit of a relative few?

We will discuss finances later in this report. Here we are

concerned with some philosophical and social problems which only the directors of the participating libraries can finally resolve.  To help them in their decisions, I offer the following dialogue:

Q.  Why should the library try to offer a specialized information service that traditionally has never been a part of that library's functions?

A.  "Tradition" is a mis-used term.  Through the years libraries have constantly changed their types and varieties of services.  At one time only the very wealthy, royal and scholarly elite enjoyed the services of libraries.  Later, libraries were limited to paying subscribers or members.

The free public library, open to all, is a relatively recent and rare phenomenon, and even during its short life the public library has made many changes in its services.  These changes are continuing. INFORM may very well mark a significant and needed change.

O.  But don't you lose the concept of the "free" public (or college) library if you start to charge for its services?

A.  No more than when the library charges for keeping materials overdue, or for motion picture rental, or for putting books on reserve. Making the library materials available to all who wish to enter and use is a great and wonderful free service.  Beyond that, there may be many reasons and instances when a fee is justified.  This will vary with libraries, according to their own views of their responsibilities and their budgets.

Q.  But don't both public and academic libraries have other responsibilities which could come first?

A.  Yes.  Unless some very drastic changes are made, public libraries always will offer free service to the general public on its usual basis.  And college libraries will see their primary function to support the school's curriculum and research needs.  But neither one should feel that this is the limit of what they can do.  Many studies indicate that a very small part of the general public makes intensive use of their libraries, and the use by students is not what it should be for their best education.  One study found many faculty members were unaware of basic library services, such as reference and inter-library loan, did not understand the purpose of a union catalog, and some did not know the difference between a card catalog and a computer-generated book catalog.[8]

And when the University of California (Berkeley) library ran a simple experiment on campus delivery service, 54% of the users reported it changed their library use habits (for the better).  Sample comment: "Because the library is now easier to use, my usage has increased."[9]

INFORM might produce similar types of change in use by students and faculty.  Most college libraries are familiar with student and faculty attitudes that say:

"I can expect to locate only about half the items I am looking for."

"I can never find anything I really need . . ."

"Nothing you ever want is properly shelved . . ."

Information service for a fee might create new users among those who have been turned off by their former frustrations and defeats when trying to use the college library. ("75% of the students admitted confusion in their use of libraries, especially the University library, and only 2% of the confused turned to the librarian for assistance.")[10]

The responses of INFORM's customers indicate that most knew very little about the many fine services available free from the various libraries. Many inquiries for INFORM service might be handled without charge by another department of the library. And INFORM's aggressive program for seeking new customers will help publicize library service in general.

Q. What happens if the customer asks for information or service that is totally beyond the library's ability to deliver?

A. INFORM's record to date suggests that this would be a very rare event and would be no blight on INFORM's reputation if it should occur. Once, when it did happen, the client was happy to learn nothing could be found. It was just what he wanted to know.[11]

Our interviews and other experience show the opposite--patrons are more often amazed at how much good information can be quickly produced by an intensive search by a dedicated professional librarian. There is a potential benefit from the challenge of INFORM-type questions. It could show weaknesses in the library's collection or indexes which, when amended to serve INFORM, would make the library more useful to all users.

INFORM could also offer a challenging goal for staff members who are ambitious to do in-depth reference work.

Q. Is it possible that INFORM might become too popular--that it might develop more business than it can handle?

A. 'Tis a consummation devoutly to be wished. Although the growth trend has been steep in INFORM's first 3 years, in coming years it should be gradual enough to allow planning and preparation for expanded use. If the use of INFORM continues to grow, it confirms what we have been saying--that there is a great need for this type of service. Economies of scale say that as the number of questions rises, the costs per question tend to go down. The day might come when every businessman in the Twin Cities made some use of INFORM. Would this not create a better appreciation for all the services of these libraries and stimulate greater use (and greater support) for them? A hypothetical and unanswerable question now, but not one to fear.

The justification for a special library does not hinge on statistics--the number of books added, reports cataloged or questions answered. These might indicate how busy the library is, but they don't say much about its value to the organization paying its bills. Management wants to know, "What are we getting for our dollars?" And the best answer is for management to have a clear understanding and firm conviction about the value of information service, how it saves time and money, prevents wasted effort and duplication, stimulates the creation of better products, processes, and procedures, helps make better decisions and helps individuals keep up with new developments. A "management" which has seen the results when its information problems are answered quickly, completely, specifically, professionally, will have little trouble justifying the place (or budget) of its information service.

## Financing

This part of the report should have perhaps come first, because without the money to operate INFORM, all other questions are pointless.

Many sad stories have been told about library projects or programs which promised great and valuable benefits, but then foundered for lack of adequate dollars.  TIS (Technical Information Services) was one such program, although out of it grew services like MINITEX, SMU's Industrial Information Services and Georgia Tech's Information Exchange Center.

But money is a fact of life.  And if we are convinced that good information service has a genuine and practical dollars and cents value, we should be able to market a service that is truly viable, i.e., "capable of living, capable of growing and developing a life of its own, self-supported."  Does information have real value?  Is it worth dollars and cents?  Let us look at a few graphic examples:

"In 1962 the 3M company sued Ditto, Inc. for infringing on 3M's patents covering the Thermofax copying process.  In court, Ditto produced an English translation of an 1859 French technical paper which described the concept of thermography.  On the basis of this information, the court ruled that 3M's patent was invalid and Ditto, Inc. was not infringing."

"3M won a new trial when it discovered the original and more complete French paper and convinced the court that the older translations had stressed a different process from that used by Thermofax."[12]

How much was that information worth?

In 1973, Control Data Corporation won an out-of-court settlement of its suit against IBM estimated to be worth as much as $250 million.  Why did CDC win?  Why did IBM give up without going to court?  "Because CDC had come up with a secret weapon that others could use against IBM as well--including Telex and the Federal government, which had filed an antitrust suit against the giant."[13]

This secret weapon was a computerized index to some 750,000 pages of IBM documents, 100,000 pages of CDC documents and tens of thousands of other documents from other sources, all related to matters in the suit.  Total cost to prepare this index (estimated):  $1.5 million.

Under the terms of the settlement, CDC agreed to destroy this index.  Telex and the U.S. government immediately filed suit claiming that CDC had destroyed evidence and asking that the index be restored and made available to them.  The court ruled that CDC had destroyed no evidence, only their own index to the evidence, and that Telex and the government were free to make their own index, as CDC had done.

How much was this index to information worth to Control Data?

On a smaller scale--Cargill, Inc. wanted to know if they could substitute fish oil (at 27¢ per pound) for linseed oil (at 45¢ per pound)

in their urethane resin products.  A literature search found a report of
work done in India on this very problem, indicating that such substitution was possible.  Cargill's director of resin research estimated
that this information saved at least 3 man month's research and testing,
plus the value of all savings realized by the substitution.  Plus the
value of work that could be done by those who were released from this
problem.

Information does have a definite, practical dollars and cents
value.  INFORM's customers have testified to that.  Thus, INFORM has the
opportunity to tap a large and waiting market for information service
for-a-fee.

But will this market be large enough to let INFORM balance its
budget?  No one knows.  It has to be tried.  Other problems also have
to be considered.

1) Can INFORM depend on additional support or seed money from the
federal or state governments?

2) How well can INFORM analyze its true costs, so that it knows
exactly how much (if any) subsidy comes from the regular library
budgets?  (If a private agency took over INFORM, what would their
costs be?)

3)  How can INFORM decide how much of such a subsidy is tolerable,
justifiable?  Earlier we mentioned the possibility that INFORM's activities might bring benefits to the regular library operations as a
trade-off.

4)  Where is the point of diminishing return, if INFORM should
raise its fees?  (Very few customers thought the fee high; many said it
could be higher.)

5)  How can INFORM estimate its costs and receipts a year or two in
advance, in order to make proper plans for proper service?  (One customer suggests:  "They should budget on an annual basis, like a church--
run it for a year and see how you come out, then adjust for the next
year.")

6) How busy does INFORM want to be?  If the number of searching
hours in 1974 goes to 1,000 (from 762 in 1973), this would bring in
$18,000.  How close would that be to making INFORM self-supporting?
Where would the break-even point be?

7) Would the National Commission on Libraries and Information
Centers be interested in the INFORM experiment?  Would they be willing
to help with a subsidy in order to thoroughly test this new concept in
public library service?

8) INFORM offers a rare chance for a library truly to test the value
of its services in the most realistic way in the market place where the
Customer is King, where any service survives and prospers only so long as
customers remain satisfied with the service and show it by buying it
repeatedly.


## The Future for INFORM

Does INFORM have a future?  INFORM has a great future, depending on
some vital IFS and BUTS.  For some perspective, let us look back a bit.

Thirty years ago a young special librarian, fresh out of library
school, was trying to provide a total information service to a large

Twin Cities advertising firm. His patrons were artists, designers, writers and other operative personnel, sales managers, salesmen and sales promotion staff, market and technical researchers, administrative and production people.

Very often he had to reach outside his small collection for needed information. This meant guessing which Twin City library might have what was needed, traveling to that library and searching its collection. No photocopy facilities were available then.

If he found some relevant information, he had to charge the material out and bring it back to his library, there to re-charge it to his patron, later to retrieve it and return it to its source. The material might be available for one month, one week, one day or over-night; or it might not circulate at all. He then had to copy (by hand) or summarize its contents.

If he did not find what he needed, he had to move to another library and repeat his search. He could easily spend an entire day looking for the answers to only a few problems. Meanwhile, he was away from his desk, unavailable to his own patrons.

Today that same librarian provides a total information service for another corporation, also with wide interests and the need for prompt, accurate information service. Without leaving his desk, that librarian now can locate sources quickly and easily; through MULS (and other serials holdings lists) he has at his fingertips (by phone) some 50,000 to 60,000 journals in all subject fields, many languages. He can have photocopies made and mailed to reach him within one or two days (sooner, if necessary). If what he needs is not in the MULS list, he can ask to have it located elsewhere.

Photocopies also will be made from books, government documents and other sources. Books will be identified, located, borrowed and mailed promptly and conveniently.

But even more than that, this librarian, if he has problems beyond his ability to solve, or if he is too busy to search for it or needs the information in a very short time, can phone any of 4 libraries and ask for help. He will explain his problem, define his needs, declare his deadline and specify how much the information is worth to him on the basis of $18 for each hour spent in searching for it. He then can go back to his other work, available to his patrons for discussion and more questions.

In short, he can, at a moment's notice, add to his staff on an hourly basis, the services of competent, dedicated, experienced librarians, familiar with the extensive sources of their large libraries.

What he receives is a searching service that is as good as or better than he could do himself. He will save the time he would have to spend in traveling, searching, charging out or making photocopies.

That librarian now can accomplish as much in one 8 hour day as formerly might take an entire week. This is great progress.

Three main elements have made this progress possible. The first and most important is Commitment. The decision to establish INFORM was based on the belief that Information is a valuable resource, that a specialized information service was a worthwhile venture, badly needed and with no other agency capable of providing it. Along with this belief went the sense of commitment to the goal of "access to library resources and professional skills to a degree not available through ordinary reference service."

The second is technology. Photocopy makes information available to everyone without depriving anyone. Computers produce multiple copies of union catalogs and serials lists, and can keep them revised and up to date rapidly, accurately: computers also can store huge amounts of information and produce any part of the store quickly on demand, even at long distances. Microforms allow great savings in cost and space. They enable many libraries to have and hold rare and unusual materials that otherwise would be beyond their means.

The third is people. In spite of all the wonders of modern science, people still are the priceless ingredient. The customer does not talk or write to an institution, but to another human being. This individual has to be a rare combination of counselor, consultant, professional librarian and problem solver. Such individuals are not easily found, or trained. Rowena Swanson sums it up:

"The attainment of interactive, productive relationships with user groups is a gradual, up-hill process, mostly because of person-to-person communication problems and the lack of adequately trained personnel, rather than financial or other insufficiencies. Change agents capable of performing these varied tasks are in short supply."[14]

Thus, INFORM struggles with problems that are very basic, very normal, and very much human. People need information but they often do not realize they need it. If they realize it, they often have difficulty describing what they need. If they know what they need, they may have no idea where to turn to find what they need. If they know where to turn, they may not be competent to do their own searching efficiently. If they do their own searching, they may fall victim to Swanson's "Fallacy of abundance."[15]

Finally, and to ring our theme just one more time, no one can know how much any bit of information may be worth until after he has been able to use it. Perhaps not even then. So how can someone determine in advance before he even sees what information is available, how much he should spend to search for it? And yet, every day, individuals are spending great sums of time and energy searching for information or trying to do without it, or of being forced to do work inefficiently because they do not have it.

It is my firm conviction that this is a very important matter, and that INFORM has made a good start toward improving the situation.

If information is valuable (and I believe it is), and if the right information is difficult to find (and it usually is for the non-librarian), then the more that INFORM is used for its searching capabilities, the more the user will benefit, the more his organization will benefit, and the more we will all benefit.

This puts a great responsibility on the directors of INFORM. They are not only in the business of answering questions for a fee. But they also have the problem of making graphic the value of INFORM's specialized no-limit service; they have the problem of finding and

training the individuals who will be highly competent, not only professionally and technically, but in the ability to create a feeling of
confidence and trust among the users of INFORM.

INFORM has and will continue to have problems.  INFORM needs to
advertise its services much more widely, much more effectively than it
has.  It must explore many avenues for publicity and advertising--
direct mail, newspapers, magazines, radio, TV, and personal appear-
ances--to make more people aware of INFORM and what it can do to help
them.

INFORM will have a great future--

IF the directors of INFORM will hold to their conviction that a
specialized information service is valuable, is needed, is worthwhile
and offers a direct and broad benefit to our community.

IF the directors see INFORM as a logical and added dimension to
traditional services provided by public (and academic) libraries.

IF the directors can find ways to make INFORM approach a self-
supporting basis.  Again, quoting Rowena Swanson:  "Sales of a product
on a free market are a measure of the product's worth to the customers."  And Campbell:  "How can the operators of an information
service know if the service is meeting its responsibilities?  By giving
thoughtful attention to expressed and behavioral reactions of the
users."[16]

This brings us back to our original thesis:  To evaluate INFORM,
we must look into the horse's mouth--the user and his needs.  What we
see is mostly positive.  Today, through INFORM, we have an organized,
systematic, responsive network that offers fine information service for
a fair fee.  We who, day in and day out, struggle with this responsibility recognize INFORM as a great boon and bargain.  Read again the
words of the special librarian who said:

"None of us could survive without using other resources.  INFORM
has been really great for us, especially in areas where our collection just wasn't good enough for the kinds of questions we were
getting."

Peering into the future, we can see some of these pros and cons for
INFORM:

## Advantages (fee system)

Increased use of the libraries by private organizations, individuals, professionals, with a resulting greater awareness of the library's
facilities and capabilities.

Reasonable way to handle proprietary interests of users.

Means for determining if such a service is needed and has a value
which can be self-supporting.

Demonstrate to other library organizations the value, validity and
feasibility of this type of service.

Reveal needed resources in the library collection which then are
available to all patrons.

Provide training ground for personnel to experience the problems and challenges of "the market place," where satisfying the needs of the customer are the goal and criterion.

## Disadvantages

Billing problems associated with fee payment service.
Possible shift of service emphasis to those who can pay for it.
Possible legal problems related to performing a "public" free service for a fee.
May become a form of subsidization to commercial private interests.
May develop possible competition (envy, jealousy, tension) between INFORM and other traditionally non-fee areas of the libraries.
(Adapted from "The Marketing of Information Analysis Center Products and Services," by Walter H. Yeazie, Jr. and Thomas F. Connolly, June 1971, ERIC Clearinghouse on Library and Information Sciences, Washington, D.C.)

## References

1. Buckley, William. New Yorker 47:40 (Aug. 28, 1971).

2. Drucker, Peter. "The Age of Discontinuity." N.Y., Harper & Row 1969, pp. xi, 27.

3. Dodd, James B. "Pay-as-you-go plan for satellite industrial libraries using academic facilities." Special Lib. 64: 66-72 (Feb. 1974).

4. White, Herbert S. "Special librarianship--the special one is the customer!" Minnesota Libraries 21 (12):339-346 (Dec. 1966).

5. Mueller, Max. "Time, cost and value factors in information retrieval." In Information Retrieval Systems Conference, Poughkeepsie, N.Y., 1959. General Information Manual (papers) N.Y. IBM Corp., 1959.

6. Munn, Robert F. "The Bottomless Pit, or The Academic Library as viewed from the Administration Building." College & Res. Lib. 29: 51-54 (Jan. 1968).

7. Goddard, Haynes C. "An economic analysis of library benefits." Library Q. 41(3): 244-255 (July 1971).

8. Leonard, L.E. et al. Centralized processing: a feasility study based on Colorado academic libraries. Metuchen, N.J., Scarecrow Press, Inc. 1969.

9. Dougherty, Richard M. "The evaluation of campus library document delivery service." College & Res. Lib. 34: 29-39 (Jan. 1973).

10.  Amundson, Colleen C.  "Relationships between University freshmen's information-gathering techniques and selected environmental factors."  Unpublished Ph.D. Thesis, Univ. of Minn., 1971.

11.  INFORM Newsletter, vol. 1, no. 1 (May 1972).

12.  St. Paul Dispatch, April 19, 1963 "Business News" section; and Chemical & Engineering News, p. 26, Sept. 14, 1964.

13.  Newsweek, p. 82, October 1, 1973; and New York Times, Feb. 6, 1973.

14.  Swanson, Rowena W.  "Information--an Exploitable Commodity." U.S. Govt. Res. Report AD 677-197, April, 1968.  Available from the National Technical Information Service, Washington, D.C.

15.  Swanson, Don R.  "Searching natural language text by computer." Science 132:  1099-1104 (Oct. 21, 1960).  "Who nowadays imagines that he can find in the library whatever he may have missed when it was first published is a victim of 'the fallacy of abundance.' Because so much is found is no guarantee that the best for his needs is found.  All indexes and catalogs are imperfect."

16.  Campbell, Wayne R.  "Feedback from the user--sine qua non" in Howerton, Paul W. ed., Information Handling:  First Principles Washington, D.C.  Spartan Books, 1963, pp. 107-108.

# COMMENTARY ON
# THE SPECIAL LIBRARIAN/FEE-BASED SERVICE INTERFACE

by

Nancy M. Kingman
3M Business Library

and

Carol Vantine
Minneapolis Public Library

It has been a practice, in other times, for drinking emporiums to hang signs advertising, and consequently offering, a free lunch. The catch is that one eating said free lunch pays through the nose for the liquid accompaniments and leaves with a lunch "free" in name only.[1] You pay for what you get.

Special librarians are part of an industry that is just being recognized as an industry and one that is still suffering the pangs of generation, organization, and development. Information is a resource, just like fuel or other raw materials. Corporations and other businesses are just beginning to treat information in this way and to plan for its supply or evaluate the impact of neglecting the demands for it within their corporate sphere. It is our responsibility as professionals to be sure that our segment of this industry--people giving data to people--maintains the quality of our product, information. For if the quality of data provided to business fails as a result of poorly conducted searches for outdated source material, all librarians suffer from the resultant diminished credibility. Business people _are_ demanding more and better data with which to make decisions.[2] The Minneapolis Public Library and several other public institutions[3] offer fee-based services such as INFORM[4] to meet this demand, to acquire and maintain access to specialized collections, and to provide high-quality contractual (and therefore confidential) service.

## Need for Fee-Based Services

Proponents of the sanctity of special libraries argue that each library will build its own superlative collection and operate independently, hence having no need for fee-based service. Yet, with information in technical areas projected to double approximately every four years,[5] an internal, complete collection is not only unrealistic and

unreasonable, but an economically ineffectual goal.  In subject areas
where demands are infrequent or collections are already in existence
somewhere else, it is cheaper and quicker to use the already established collection and to use it through someone with day-to-day
knowledge of that collection.  We are all proud of our own special
expertise, but each of us is limited.  We need to rely on others when
they have something unique to offer.

Many corporate clients come directly to INFORM for their informational needs, bypassing their company libraries for one of a number
of reasons.  The business person may think that the special librarian
is too busy or not concerned enough with the nature and urgency[6]
(whether real or imagined) of his or her problem.  He or she may feel
that the library's resources are too specialized or not specialized
enough to be of help, or may be unaware that the company even has a
librarian to help with informational needs.  If the special librarian
is being bypassed, serious questions about the role of the corporate
librarian should be raised.

INFORM does not aspire to replace any librarian, but rather to
support and supplement the librarian's resources when the occasion is
appropriate.  The business person does not care how the answers are
obtained, only that the information is accurate, pertinent, and provided quickly.  The crucial point is, however, that it is the corporate
librarian who can best assess the nature of the question in the context
of the company and evaluate the immediate resources at hand and the
potential resources of fee-based services such as INFORM, to determine
the most efficient and fruitful steps to take.  It should be the professional judgment of the librarian to decide that an outside agency can
conduct the search most efficiently because of its special skills or
because it possesses a useful anonymity that is necessary to protect
the interests of the company.  The requestor will remember only  excellent service.  The librarian's position in the corporate structure is
strengthened by interfacing the decision maker with the relevant information; and services like INFORM gain professional support, respect and
cooperation.

## Call for Cooperation

Cooperation is an often heard word these days, but one that does
not fully define the present relationship between special librarians
and fee-based research services.  INFORM, located in the central branch
of the Minneapolis Public Library, has access to an excellent collection
on its own premises, but to be effective, must access academic,
research, and private libraries as well as contact trade associations,
experts in specialized fields, companies, or any other source anywhere
in the world to provide accurate information.  Often, it is a corporate
library somewhere in the United States that owns the particular journal
that will facilitate INFORM's search.  Their cooperation in supplying
non-proprietary information enables INFORM to do a better job and provides some mechanism for repayment to the loaner.  When the librarian
at Amalgamated Widget calls, Acme Widget is usually willing to help,
but repetitive requests for photocopy can become a burden on good will.
A middle service can facilitate such requests by plugging into the most

accessible collection (stressing those that are public) and relying on private collections only if necessary.

It is this cooperation and support that gives special librarians a degree of control over the quality of information that is distributed by our mutual industry and allows enforcement of a high standard for the searches performed. Every community should have an INFORM-type service available to provide the corporate librarian with a face-to-face tie-in to the broad informal network of public and private information sources across the United States. Only if all segments of the information industry maintain high standards can our professional group gain stature and respect as well as increase the demand for all our various information services. Those such as INFORM are the special librarian's legs, eyes, and brain when he or she needs them. Not to use INFORM-type operations or to encourage other such services to be established in many localities is to narrow the scope of service that a librarian can offer his or her institution. When Avis began its extensive "we try harder" campaign, they were not able to change their position in the car rental market. The campaign was responsible, however, for a tremendous boom in the car rental business as a whole and better service from all the component companies.[7] The same can and will occur within the information industry if every business community will become more and more reliant upon those who can supply its needs.

## The Special Librarian as Consumer Advocate

Part of the payment for good fee-based service must be the force of the special librarian as consumer advocate. Special librarians have to demand a good quality of work and to expose and publicize poor quality, because all information service, fee-based or "free," is a reflection on the entire industry. Thus, each of us needs to assume a watchdog role in relation to new entries into our field. This has to be a professional responsibility. We cannot afford to let outsiders establish standards for the quality of work that is a part of, and reflects on, the totality of our industry.

Librarians must also demand a system whereby local service is integrated and compatible with other services across the country and even worldwide. For example, the Business Information Service at 3M can utilize INFORM so well because it is not hindered by long distance phone calls, lengthy correspondence, or a name and a voice with no face. 3M and INFORM are familiar with each others' proficiency, collection, goals--and shortcomings. But 3M needs to tap into a whole system through one contact. The company will lose what has been gained through cooperation if the librarian has to spend whole days on the phone. The need for an integrated U.S. network of fee-based services is real--it is preferable to see a strong network grow as a result of a professional demand rather than have a wide variety of noncooperating services grow as a result of corporate librarians' failure to recognize corporate information needs.

## In Conclusion

And now, a second law of economics--the rich get richer and the poor get poorer.[8] The corporate librarian who interacts with the relevant and reliable fee-based services gets richer--in the sense that he or she is providing the requestor with the best available information, regardless of whether it is in-house or not. And as we all know, good information is addictive to the receiver. And the poor, for whatever reason, are providing their requestors with a diet lean in information calories--and not stimulating the appetite for more. We are all accountable for our professional existence, and our success can be measured in the support (or lack of it) provided by corporate management.

In summary, if you are less than satisfied with the service you've been providing; or you are more overworked than usual and can't see your way out--take an information broker to lunch.

## Literature Cited

1. Friedman, Milton / There's No Such Thing As a Free Lunch. La Salle, Ill., Open Court Publishing Co., 1975.

2. de Carbonnel, Francois and Roy G. Dorrance / Information Sources for Planning Decisions. California Management Review XV (4):42-53 (Summer 1973).

3. For example: the Center for Research, Inc., University of Kansas, Lawrence, Kans.; the Information Exchange Center, Georgia Institute of Technology, Atlanta, Ga.; the Technical and Business Information Service sponsored by the Rochester, N.Y.; and the Business Information Service, Houston Public Library, Houston, Texas.

4. Shannon, Zella / Public Library Service to the Corporate Community. Special Libraries 65 (no. 1): 12-26 (Jan. 1974).

5. Big Growth Ahead in Technical Information. Chemical and Engineering News 51:7 (Apr. 23, 1973).

6. Johnson, Rita M. / Interviews with marketing personnel, 3M Company, St. Paul, Minn., Sep. 1975.

7.  Now Avis Thinks it Can Become No. 1.  Business Week (Feb. 6,
    1971).


8.  Kahn, Gus and Raymond B. Egan (lyrics) and Richard A. Whiting
    (music) / Ain't We Got Fun.  New York, Jerome H. Remick and Co.,
    1921.

# PLANNING FOR ON-LINE SEARCH
# IN THE PUBLIC LIBRARY

by

Oscar Firschein and Roger K. Summit
Lockheed Palo Alto Research Laboratory

and

Colin K. Mick
Applied Communication Research, Inc.

The DIALIB project involved an experiment in placing retrieval terminals in four public libraries in Northern California. After three years of experience, in which patrons were provided with free search for one year, one-half priced search for the second year, and full fee search in the third year, the authors delineate the requirements for online search and formulate guidelines useful for public libraries contemplating one search service.

The first year of the DIALIB experiment, which investigated on-line search in the public library, was discussed in an article in Special Libraries (1). The DIALIB experiment, has since been described in several reports (2-5). Briefly, four libraries in Northern California, members of the Cooperative Information Network (CIN), were selected to participate, and Lockheed Information Systems provided the project coordination and the DIALOG retrieval service. The study was evaluated by Applied Communication Research, a nonprofit behavioral research firm in Palo Alto, Calif. Some of the goals of the experiment were to investigate the usefulness of on-line search to the public, to determine the impact of on-line search on the library, and to determine whether the public was willing to pay part or all of the costs. Based on the results obtained, one of the main products of the study was the development of guidelines that would be useful for libraries contemplating on-line search service.

## Use of On-Line Search

The authors found that the traditionally trained public librarian does have a variety of skills that are directly applicable to the kinds of skills required in on-line searching. These include the ability to form an adequate search query by consulting with the user and

encouraging the user to communicate his needs fully.  The traditionally
trained reference librarian is already expert with complex manual
tools--thesauri, indexes, and others--and the skills developed with
these tools are transferable to computer data base searching.  There is
considerable evidence that traditional reference librarians are willing
and able to learn data base search techniques.  In fact, many
librarians involved in DIALIB became skilled on-line searchers.

There appear to be two problems.  The first is training on specific data bases and subject skills.  The second problem area has to
do with subject expertise.  For research queries of greater complexity
than "simple fact" questions, many people feel that the searcher should
be a subject expert.  If a library does not have a subject specialist
(e.g., science, technology, business), then this problem can be at
least partially resolved by having the patron present for the search.
(This assumes, of course, that the patron has some knowledge of the
search topic area.)

In general, there appear to be few precise reference/information
policies in public libraries which establish limits in terms of
services offered, topics covered, patron eligibility, and allocation
of staff time.  Public libraries have been able to live with informal
limits because the demands placed upon reference service have not been
that great.  One major result of the DIALIB experiment has been to
focus attention on the reference function in the public library (6).

## Key Requirements for On-Line Search

Using the findings given in the Evaluation Annex to the final
report (5), a set of guidelines have been formulated for use by public
libraries contemplating on-line search service.*  Nine key requirements
were identified.

## Establishing Scope and Limits of Service

The first key requirement for a public library offering on-line
searching is to define the scope and limits of service.  Every library
has some set of rules to define scope and service.  Some rules are
explicit, such as requiring cards to check out books.  Other rules are
implicit, for example, decisions as to how much time to devote to a
particular type of question, such as a phone question.  In addition,
the library can also limit service without rules--by not making people
aware of the service.

In offering on-line searching, the library must invest significant
effort into establishing the scope and limits of the service.  Issues
which must be dealt with include:
   • What are the goals and objectives of the service?
   • Will the service be used to support internal operations, to
provide service to patrons, or both?

---

*A recent publication by the American Library Association (7) should
also be consulted.

• What limits should be established in terms of subject areas, costs, and staff time?
• Will user fees be used to limit service?
• Who will be allowed access to the service?
• When will the service be available?
• What kind of service will be provided?
• What level of publicity will be used?

These are major questions. Determining the scope and limits of the service has major impact on other decisions which must be made. It is important that the service should be structured by the goals and objectives of the library and the needs of its patrons, not by the potential of on-line searching.

## Staff Time Requirements

The staff time requirements associated with the introduction and provision of on-line searching cannot be overemphasized. Throughout the DIALIB experiment, staff time was perceived by the libraries to be the major inhibiting factor. Searches average approximately one hour of staff time (for query negotiation, search preparation, searching, and post-search activities). In addition, time is required for promotion, accounting, and training of search personnel.

Libraries planning to introduce on-line searching must very carefully consider the impact on their staff. They must be prepared to add staff to support the new service or to divert staff from other activities if and when user demand develops.

## Staff Attitudes and Support

Preconceptions and attitudes of library personnel toward fee-based service, and the role of reference services, play a great part in determining the direction and ultimate success of on-line searching.

More specifically, the attitudes and support of the head reference librarian and the library director are crucial to the success of on-line searching. Unless both are firmly committed to work for and support on-line searching, the probability for success is at best marginal.

The attitudes and support of the reference librarians who will serve as searchers are also important. However their reactions toward on-line searching in the public library will be determined, to a large extent, by the activities and opinions of the head reference librarian and the library director.

In developing a plan for on-line searching, it is vital that emphasis be placed on establishing and maintaining the support of the library staff--from the administration to the reference service to the circulation department.

## Funding

The financial requirements for on-line searching can be divided into three categories:
1) Capital (startup) costs include initial training, initial

purchase of a computer terminal (if the terminal is purchased),
purchase of documentation, and initial training costs.

2) Marginal (or variable) costs are those costs that can be associated with a specific search.  They include retrieval service costs
(based on terminal connect time and printing charges), communication
costs, and search-related staff time.

3) Overhead charges are those charges that are specific to the
on-line search service but cannot be associated with any specific
search.  These may include terminal rental (if the terminal is leased),
terminal maintenance (included in the leasing cost), staff time for
training (and also search-related staff time if not charged as a
marginal cost), maintenance of documentation, and maintenance of training.  Errors in searching can also be considered as an overhead cost.

Some specific cost values will clarify the subsequent discussion.
The Cooper-DeWath study (5) shows an average cost of a search during
the pay period as $26.44, including off-line and on-line staff time and
search service cost (connect time and printouts).  If we assume 30
searches per month, we obtain the figures in Table 1.

Table 1
Monthly Cost of On-Line Searching

| (30 searches/month) | ($26.44 per search) | | | = $ 800 |
|---|---|---|---|---|
| (30 searches/month) | (1/4 hour connect time) | ($8 per hour) communication cost* | | = $ 60 |
| Terminal cost per month, including maintenance | | | | = $ 125 |
| | | Total monthly cost | | $1000 (approx) |

If we assume an annual budget of $500 for staff training, $500 for
reference materials, and $500 for publicity, we see that the annual
cost of an on-line search service performing 30 searches per month is
$13,500.

A public library has the option of either supporting this cost from
the library budget or grants, and offering the service to the public at
no cost; or service can be offered at a fee that partially or completely
covers the cost.  If the service is supported by the library budget,
then the library must develop policies which define and limit the services provided.  In the free portion of the DIALIB project, the
libraries did not place overt limits on the service.  When they were
confronted by rapidly increasing search requests, they opted for an
implicit form of control—cutting off all publicity about the service.
The lack of specific policies and rules for the on-line search service
had a continued impact on the DIALIB project.  This is an area which

---

*Most major cities in the U.S. have Tymnet or Telenet communications
service to the search services at $8/hour or less.

should be of prime concern regardless of whether the service is offered on a free or pay basis: the establishment of the scope and limits of service, as discussed previously, is strongly related to the funding question.

## Need for Promotional Planning

Promotional planning is an essential part of the development of the on-line search service. Failure to promote the service will keep it from reaching its full potential. Printed signs, brochures and public announcement can be effective. However, demonstrations of on-line searches to potential users has been found to be one of the most effective ways of publicizing the capabilities of on-line searching. Small, portable terminals are now available that allow off-site demonstrations to be given to school, community, and business groups.

## Need for Ongoing Staff Training

The library must also invest in ongoing searcher training on data bases. The search services generally offer one- and two-day training sessions in the use of their systems, and training in the use of specific data bases is generally offered by the data base producers.

Lack of specific data base training was a common complaint among librarians across all libraries and all three years of the project. In obtaining specific data base training, the library will confront three problems:

• Availability of training. Data base providers generally offer training sessions only a few times a year in various parts of the country.

• Availability of personnel. Sending librarians to training presents a staff cost expense to the library.

• Training costs. Many data base providers charge for training sessions and, unless the sessions are available locally, training may require travel and per diem costs.

## Need for a Critical Mass of Searches

A critical mass of searches is required to maintain searcher competence. Most librarians interviewed agreed that five to 10 searches per month were necessary to maintain search skills for each data base. Certainly it is possible to conduct searches on a less frequent basis; however, the librarians indicated that they felt under these circumstances they were less efficient.

Search competence is concerned with specific data bases rather than general skills required to deal with the search system. This suggests that rather than have one or two searchers handling all searches, it would be more effective to train a number of searchers and have each specialize in only a few data bases.

Centralized searching for a library network, or a library system with branches, is feasible. Data show little difference in client satisfaction with results when the search is negotiated at a branch rather than the searching library. The data also show, however, that branch

libraries in San Mateo County sent in few searches. Thus, although
maintenance of a centralized search facility may provide the necessary
critical mass, careful attention must be paid to training and working
with branch librarians in order to have the branches forward questions
to the search center. Training should include familiarity with the
on-line search service, an awareness of available data bases, and query
negotiation.

## Document Support

To provide effective searching, the library must be prepared to
invest in and maintain adequate support documentation, such as thesauri.
Documentation is required for the search services and for each individual data base. Some of this documentation is available free of
charge; however, some must be purchased. Document cost for each data
base used ranges from a low of $10 to $15 to a high of over $100.

There is a need for better data base documentation, search service
documentation, and summary documentation, and such documentation must
be periodically revised and kept up-to-date. In particular, we need:
brief data base guides, as well as detailed data base descriptions;
guides that show similar search commands in each major service; documentation that compares data base characteristics along common dimen-
sions, such as language, scope, or types of documents included and
excluded; tabular and summary documentations and comparisons for
at-terminal use. Some work has been done in this area (for example, by
the National Federation of Abstracting and Indexing Services and by the
American Society for Information Science), but more is needed.

## Management and Evaluation

Another area which libraries should explore carefully is management
and evaluation, particularly in accounting for staff time. It is essential that accurate data be collected to allow the library administrator
to assess the impact of the search service on the public and on the
library. This requires the establishment and maintenance of detailed
procedures for recording staff time and activities.

If the service is to be offered on a fee basis, then additional
procedures are required to govern the collection of funds. If the
service is offered via a network, then it is important that a single,
uniform system be developed to transmit requests to the searching
library and to transmit search results back to the requesting library or
to the patron.

Evaluation is extremely important. This includes evaluation of
impact on the library, user impact, and the quality of the searches produced. It is essential that some procedure be developed to collect user
feedback to assist in the evaluation. Unfortunately, procedures for
assessing the quality of searches are still ad hoc in nature, and
research remains to be done in this area.

## Conclusions

A member of the DIALIB Oversight Committee, Douglas Ferguson, has commented on the project as follows:

"The same constraints and choices apply to traditional reference service as apply to computer-supported reference service.
When the similarities rather than the differences are emphasized,
a price-free service structure can be made to work. The false
dilemma that plagued the thinking of many of us, and I emphasize
that this included myself, was not free vs. fee service, but total
vs. balanced access to service. No library offers unlimited
access to its resources or facilities. Every library chooses
what sources, how much staff time and talent and what access conditions it will offer to the public--and so does virtually every
other public service organization. . . . It seems to me that
what results from these choices is a type of service that balances
available resources across a spectrum of library services (4,
Appendix G)."

In this paper the authors have tried to indicate the questions
that will have to be answered by public librarians contemplating the
addition of on-line search services in order to integrate such service
into the existing library structure.

## Acknowledgments

The project, supported by the Division of Science Information,
National Science Foundation, under Grant DS174-13972-A02, could not
have been carried out without the hard work and cooperation of the
participating CIN libraries (San Jose Public Library, Redwood City
Public Library, San Mateo County Library, and Santa Clara County
Library at Cupertino). The authors also wish to thank the Oversight
Committee (consisting of Charles Bourne, Forrest F. Carhart, Jr.,
Douglas Ferguson, Virginia Ross Geller, and Albert H. Rubenstein) for
their counsel and guidance.

Table 2
A Checklist of Questions for Use as a Planning Guide

1) Should we offer on-line search service?
   • What goals will we attain by offering this service?
   • Do we have experience in in-depth reference service?
   • Do we have a potential user group?
   • Is the staff positive toward offering such service?
   • Are the data bases offered by the retrieval services
     pertinent to the needs of our patrons?
   • Can we provide adequate funds for staff, search service
     costs, and terminal by either library budget or user
     fees or a combination of both?

- If user fees seem necessary for budget support, can the fees be persuasively justified to funders, to the library staff, and to library patrons?

2) What level of service should we offer?
   - How many reference librarians can we devote to this service?
   - Do we want to actively solicit users?
   - What should our policy be for requests that come from outside of our service area, e.g., out of district users, request from other libraries?
   - Should we offer all available data bases or concentrate on just a limited number?

3) What about the details of setting up the service?
   - Should we place the terminal in an open area or do we want this to be a "back room" operation?
   - How many librarians should we train?
   - What reference aids do we want to purchase in support of the service?
   - What type of publicity should be used?
   - If a fee-for-service approach is to be used, what bookkeeping and billing arrangements are to be used?

4) How can we control the activity?
   - Do we want to prevent individuals or companies from frequent use of our service, and if so, how can this be done?
   - What records do we want to keep on search time and search activity?
   - Do we want to monitor user reaction to our on-line service?

5) How can we evaluate the effectiveness of the system?
   - What evaluation techniques can we use to obtain user reactions?
   - Can we develop a means of comparing manual and on-line search activity?
   - How can we evaluate the impact of on-line search service on the library?
   - How can we evaluate the impact of on-line search service on library users?

## Literature Cited

1. Summit, R. K. and O. Firschein / On-Line Reference Retrieval in a Public Library. Special Libraries 67 (no. 2):91-96 (Feb. 1976).

2. Summit, R. K. and O. Firschein / Two-Year Interim Report, Investigation of the Public Library as a Linking Agent to Major Scientific, Educational, Social, and Environmental Data Bases.

3 v. Oct. 1976. LMSC-D502595. Palo Alto, Calif., Information Systems Programs, Lockheed Palo Alto Research Laboratory. (ERIC ED131857, ED131858, ED131859; NTIS PD-261 858-SET/ST)

3. Ahlgren, A. E. / Project Evaluation, Annex to the Two Year Interim Report, Investigation of the Public Library as a Linking Agent to Major Scientific, Educational, Social, and Environmental Data Bases. Oct. 1976. LMSC-D502595. Palo Alto, Calif., Applied Communication Research. (ERIC ED131858)

4. Summit, R. K. and O. Firschein / Final Report, Investigation of the Public Library as a Linking Agent to Major Scientific, Educational, Social, and Environmental Data Bases. Oct. 1977. LMSC-D560986. Palo Alto, Calif., Information Systems Programs, Lockheed Palo Alto Research Laboratory. [available from NTIS as PB276726/AS (Final Report) and PB276727/AS (Evaluation Annex)].

5. Mick, C. K. / Evaluation Annex to the Final Report, Investigation of the Public Library as a Linking Agent to Major Scientific, Educational, Social, and Environmental Data Bases. Oct. 1977. LMSC-D560986. Palo Alto, Calif., Applied Communication Research. (to be available from NTIS).

6. Henne, F. E. / Comment. In The Present Status and Future Prospects of Reference Information Service. Chicago, Ill., American Library Association, 1967.

7. Watson, P. G., ed. / On-Line Bibliographic Service: Where We Are, Where We're Going. Chicago, Ill., American Library Association, Reference and Adult Services Division, Apr. 1967.

# FEES IN ACADEMIC AND SPECIAL LIBRARIES

# CHARGING POLICIES FOR ON-LINE SERVICES
# IN THE BIG TEN UNIVERSITIES

by

Sandra H. Rouse
Information Retrieval Research Laboratory
Coordinated Science Laboratory
University of Illinois at Urbana-Champaign

## Introduction

Technical services of today's large libraries are being supported by computer technology, which is generally funded by the library. A national union catalog with on-line access for librarians is available through such networks as OCLC and BALLOTS, and on-line acquisition services appeared with the development of Brodart's IROS. (1)

Use of computer technology to support public services is developing at a less rapid rate, but circulation systems, such as the CLSI network in Illinois, have been developed to facilitate interlibrary loan. (2) By identifying the location of a lending library, the patron's request for a book or journal article is satisfied. In addition, reference services are aided through on-line access to publicly available biblio-graphic data bases, which usually results in filling patrons' requests for bibliographies. For convenience, we will refer to these services as on-line reference services.

Many of the functions performed by the technical service and public service systems involve public access to published information, and therefore can be supported by computer-readable data bases, usually accessed from an on-line terminal. But one of the striking differences between technical and public services is the source of funding. Most library managers cannot justify full support of on-line reference services and thus, charge the requester all or a portion of the cost. On the other hand, such technical services as cataloging, acquisition, and circulation are not usually charged to the individual library patron. Perhaps we can attempt to identify some of the factors which influence this difference in charging policy.

Technical services support various activities that are difficult to associate with a particular patron. For example, cataloging a book will eventually result in making it available to all library users. On the other hand, public services, such as answering reference questions and circulating books, usually result from particular requests. Library managers might easily argue that those services supporting library operations, as opposed to serving the individual patron's needs, should be funded by the library budget and that a fee be charged the individual who benefits from a particular service. But it is not likely that those managers would wish to charge for every circulation. The patron does not have the choice between using a manual or an on-line circulation system, and it would be difficult to charge for use of the only available system at the library simply because it is on-line.

On the other hand, we have found that it is not unusual, at least for academic libraries, to charge their patrons for on-line reference services. (3) Unlike the circulation system, reference services provide options. The patron usually has access to Index Medicus, for example, in addition to MEDLINE. In this sense, library managers may feel that on-line reference services provide more than normal library service, especially since the patron is given a choice (i.e., his time versus his money). The result of an on-line search will provide the library patron with a tailored bibliography of references which cannot be distributed to other library patrons. In this sense, a service has been introduced that academic and public libraries traditionally have not provided.

Still, the issue of charging library patrons for services remains controversial. We have tried to identify possible justification for charging policies used in academic libraries. With approximately 360 publicly available machine-readable data bases (4) and the continued growth of on-line reference searching (5,6,7) library patrons will eventually expect this service from the library. Whether libraries will continue to charge requesters for on-line reference services is an issue to be resolved by library managers. In recognition of this issue we would like to focus on how some library managers are currently justifying their charges to patrons for on-line reference services.

Cooper and DeWath looked at the cost of on-line reference services for public libraries that changed their charging policy from free to a fee. (8) One of the interesting results of their cost study was that direct costs to the requester slightly decreased during the "pay" period because in general, less connect time was required for each search. However, librarians spent more pre- and post-search time during the "pay" period than during the free period. An important point related to the cost of on-line reference services is the amount of staff time needed to support the service. Translated into terms of the library budget, this may mean reallocating staff responsibilities and/or supporting an additional number of staff salaries.

In recognition of the current environment, where charging for on-line reference services appears to be common in academic libraries, we will attempt to identify the types of internal charging policies adopted by some academic libraries. The purpose of this paper is to describe the significant cost components of providing on-line reference service, and to discuss who pays what portion of the cost: library patron, library, university, state or federal agencies. We also identify the type of vendor contract utilized by various libraries because we recognize this as one of the factors which influences the choice of internal charging policy.

The scope of this paper is restricted to the use of on-line reference services provided by the Big Ten university libraries through the following five major vendors: BRS (Bibliographic Retrieval Services), LIS (Lockheed Information Systems), NLM (National Library of Medicine), New York Times Information Services (Information Bank), and SDC (System Development Corporation). Before we discuss the cost components of on-line reference services and the charging policies employed, we will first describe some general characteristics of the Big Ten universities.

## General Characteristics of the Big Ten Libraries

Main campuses of the Big Ten universities (see Table 1) were contacted by telephone for information regarding their on-line reference services. With the exception of two universities, on-line services are administered by the university libraries: at Indiana University, the chemistry department is responsible for providing the service, and the library at the University of Illinois holds joint responsibility with a research laboratory on that campus, the Information Retrieval Research Laboratory.

Table 1
Universities Contacted

Univ. Illinois, Urbana-Champaign
Indiana Univ., Bloomington
Univ. Iowa, Iowa City
Univ. Michigan, Ann Arbor
Michigan State Univ., East Lansing
Univ. Minnesota, St. Paul-Minneapolis
Northwestern Univ., Evanston
Ohio State Univ., Columbus
Purdue Univ., West Lafayette
Univ. Wisconsin, Madison

A very rough estimate of the volume of service provided by each campus was obtained. Each service was asked to indicate the approximate number of on-line searches provided during 1977 (see Table 2). (The reader should note that these figures were given as ball park numbers and thus should not be interpreted with a great deal of precision.) Figures given were based on either fiscal, academic, or calendar year 1977, but all represent a 12-month period roughly indicative of activity in 1977. Seven universities fall into the category of over 1,000 searches. Four of those universities (Ohio State University, the University of Michigan, the University of Minnesota, and the University of Wisconsin) indicated that roughly 3,000-4,000 was a more accurate estimate. Two responded in the range of over 100 but fewer than 500, and one university indicated a 501-1,000 range.

Rough estimates of each university's student body (i.e., undergraduate, graduate, and professional) and faculty (i.e., full-time equivalent teaching and research staff) provide some idea about the potential population served. Based on these rough estimates there is a range of 11,000 to 56,800 represented by Northwestern University and Ohio State University, respectively. The remaining universities range from 23,000 to 50,000.

To complete the general overview of the volume of service, each university estimated the percent of total searches requested by

undergraduate students, graduate students, faculty, and non-university
affiliates. In nearly all cases service to non-university requesters
is insignificant, with the exception of Ohio State University and the
University of Wisconsin, both of which estimated such searches consti-
tute 20% of the total. (Health professionals using the university's
services, when applicable, were included as faculty rather than non-
university.) Perhaps not too surprisingly, we find that at each
campus, faculty and graduate students request the majority of searches
(see Table 3).

Table 2
Number of Searches Reported

Number of searches

| 100 | none |
| 101–500 | Indiana Univ., Northwestern Univ. |
| 501–1000 | Univ. Illinois |
| 1000 | Univ. Iowa, Univ. Michigan, Michigan State Univ., Univ. Minnesota, Ohio State Univ., Purdue Univ., Univ. Wisconsin |

Table 3
Percent of Total Searches in 1977

| | Undergrad. | Grad. | Faculty | Non-university |
|---|---|---|---|---|
| Univ. Illinois | 5 | 40 | 50 | 5 |
| Indiana Univ. | 4 | 20 | 75 | 1 |
| Univ. Iowa | 5 | 70 | 22 | 3 |
| Univ. Michigan | 6 | 17 | 67 | 10 |
| Michigan State Univ. | 0 | 30 | 60 | 10 |
| Univ. Minnesota | 10 | 30 | 58 | 2 |
| Northwestern Univ. | 5 | 70 | 20 | 5 |
| Ohio State Univ. | 10 | 30 | 40 | 20 |
| Purdue Univ. | 35 | -----60------- | | 5 |
| Univ. Wisconsin | 20 | -----60------- | | 20 |

On-line Vendors and Contracts

Another aspect of the Big Ten universities' on-line reference services is the on-line systems accessed and the type of contract utilized.
A standard contract with the Information Bank, LIS, NLM, or SDC does not
require a guaranteed minimum number of dollars expended. The library
pays for connect time, telecommunications, and off-line prints on a per
unit of use basis. While LIS offers guaranteed minimum contracts none
of the libraries contacted have this type of contract with LIS.
Services from BRS are only contracted on a guaranteed minimum
basis. There are 4 different contracts offered and Table 4 indicates

which contracts apply to libraries offering BRS services.  Group
contracts for the University of Iowa and Northwestern University were
obtained through participation in MIDLNET.

### Table 4
### BRS Contracts and Universities

| | |
|---|---|
| Monthly guaranteed minimum | none |
| Annual guaranteed minimum | Michigan State Univ. |
| Group contract | Northwestern Univ., Univ. Iowa |
| Charter contract | Univ. Illinois, Univ. Minnesota, Univ. Wisconsin |

All of the universities interviewed access multiple on-line
retrieval systems.  Some of the universities may access additional
systems, such as ERDA/RECON, or have access to campus operated batch
systems.  Our overview of the universities' service is restricted to
use of the major on-line vendors.  This may not represent a total
picture of on-line service but probably represents most of the volume
of on-line searches provided.

With the exception of one university, all campuses have access to
LIS and SDC.  Services from all data bases are provided on campus except
in the case of Purdue University where Information Bank searching is
actually handled by the Indiana State Library, Reference Division.
From Table 5 we find that six of the universities access at least BRS,
six access at least NLM, and three have access to the Information Bank.

### Table 5
### Universities and On-line Vendors
### Accessed Components of Cost

| | |
|---|---|
| Univ. Illinois | BRS, LIS, SDC |
| Indiana Univ. | LIS, SDC |
| Univ. Iowa | BRS, LIS, NLM, SDC |
| Univ. Michigan | LIS, NLM, SDC |
| Michigan State Univ. | BRS, LIS, SDC |
| Univ. Minnesota | BRS, LIS, NLM, SDC |
| Northwestern Univ. | BRS, Information Bank, LIS, SDC |
| Ohio State Univ. | Information Bank, LIS, NLM, SDC |
| Purdue Univ. | Information Bank, LIS, NLM |
| Univ. Wisconsin | BRS, LIS, NLM, SDC |

The major cost components of on-line searching can be divided into
direct and indirect costs.  We should recognize the fact that direct
costs usually include staff time for organizations other than public
and academic libraries.  Library budgets, on the other hand, usually
absorb labor charges and patrons are not expected to pay for the

librarian's time.  Thus, direct and indirect costs in this discussion
are related to the management of academic library services.

Direct costs are generally the vendor's charges incurred during
the session at the terminal, while the preparatory and support activities are described as indirect costs.  We have categorized the significant indirect costs by the following:  labor, equipment, search aids,
and educational activities.  Table 6 lists the important cost components of on-line searching and from this list each university indicated the particular combination of components charged to the requester,
library, university, or some other source.

Table 6

Cost Components of On-line Searching

Direct costs

> connect time (vendor's rate, royalties)
> telecommunications
> prints, usually off-line

Indirect costs

> labor:  searcher, clerk
> equipment:  terminal, acoustic coupler, telephone,
>     paper, printer; maintenance contract/fees
> search aids:  search manuals, vocabulary aids
> education:  professional meeting participation,
>     staff training, promotional activities,
>     initial use of new search features/data bases,
>     news information

Charging Policies

A recent survey of on-line reference activity in Illinois indicated
that all academic libraries interviewed were charging their patrons for
on-line searches.  (3)  Similar results were found with this interview
of the Big Ten universities.  However, Information Bank searches are
provided free to requesters at Ohio State University and Purdue University.  In both cases, Library Services and Construction Act (LSCA) money
allocated by the respective state libraries, has been made available to
subsidize the direct costs of the search.  Indirect costs are handled
differently by these universities.  At Ohio State University the
requester obtains the Information Bank search from the reference
department and thus, the library absorbs all the indirect costs indicated in Table 6.  At Purdue University the request is sent to the
Indiana State Library where the indirect costs are thus absorbed by the
state.  At the end of this paper we will discuss some trends in charging for on-line searching and refer to the policies that guide these
free searches.

With the exception of the Information Bank searches at Ohio State

University and Purdue University, library patrons at each of the Big Ten universities are charged at least a portion of the direct costs for the on-line systems accessed. The University of Michigan is the only library to mention a state sales tax added to the cost of every search. At most universities, the requester is charged the full direct cost only; however, the charging policy usually depends on the vendor being accessed. Table 7 indicates the university-vendor combination where only direct costs are paid by the requester. Table 8 indicates the appropriate combination where the library pays a portion or all of the direct costs.

Table 7
Direct Cost of Service Paid by Requester

| University | Vendor |
| --- | --- |
| Univ. Illinois | LIS, SDC |
| Indiana Univ. | * |
| Univ. Iowa | BRS, LIS, NLM, SDC |
| Univ. Michigan | NLM |
| Michigan State Univ. | * |
| Univ. Minnesota | LIS, NLM, SDC |
| Northwestern Univ. | Information Bank, LIS, SDC |
| Ohio State Univ. | NLM, SDC |
| Purdue Univ. | LIS, NLM |
| Univ. Wisconsin | LIS, NLM, SDC |

Table 8
Subsidized Service:  Library Absorbs
Portion (or All) Direct Costs

| University | Vendor |
| --- | --- |
| Univ. Illinois | BSR |
| Indiana Univ. | * |
| Univ. Iowa | ** |
| Univ. Michigan | LIS, SDC |
| Michigan State Univ. | BRS |
| Univ. Minnesota | BRS |
| Northwestern Univ. | BRS |
| Ohio State Univ. | ** |
| Purdue Univ. | ** |
| Univ. Wisconsin | BRS |

* = charges include direct and indirect costs
** = charges include direct costs only for all vendors

To access BRS, the library must purchase service in advance of actual use.  An internal charging policy for the library patrons is based on the rate charged by BRS (dependent on the contract) and the

expected volume of use. Most libraries try to recover at least the
direct costs. However, it is possible that during some months the
library's income for the on-line service may not cover the bill for
actual use. If a deficit occurs, the library will either pay the sum
periodically (monthly, yearly, etc.), according to the contract, or
adjust their internal charging policy. We find that all libraries
offering BRS services, except the University of Iowa, describe their
charging policy for BRS services as partially subsidized by the library.
At the University of Iowa the intent (as at most of the other BRS-
contract universities) is not to subsidize the direct costs. Their
internal charging policy has so far covered actual use of the system.
Thus we see that with the guaranteed minimum contract, different
internal charging policies and higher volume of use can influence
whether or not the library subsidizes the direct costs.

All or a portion of the indirect costs are absorbed by nine of the
universities interviewed; only three universities charge their
requesters indirect costs. Indiana University is currently the only
university where the service is self-supporting and where all indirect
costs are recovered from the requester. It is also the only service
that is not affiliated with the university library. Ohio State University applies an additional $0.50 fee to LIS searches to cover the dis-
crepancy in cost estimates obtained at the terminal and the final
charge received with the vendor's bill. Any surplus revenue that might
cumulate is used by the search staff in trying new search features or
new data bases on LIS. At Michigan State University, the indirect costs
charged to the requester include equipment, search aids, and a portion
of the cost for staff attendance at professional meetings. Each search
in addition to the direct costs includes $0.18 per minute of connect
time to cover these indirect costs.

To summarize the variety of charging policies, we find that a
university may have multiple charging policies to accommodate the
different types of contracts held with multiple vendors. Eight universities charge only direct costs for at least one of the vendor services
offered (see Table 7). Three universities have adopted a charging
policy that recovers a portion or all of the indirect costs: Indiana
University (for LIS, SDC searches); Ohio State University (for LIS
searches); and Michigan State University (for BRS, LIS, SDC searches).
The University of Illinois, the University of Michigan, Michigan State
University, and the University of Minnesota charge a fixed fee for
some of their services. At the University of Illinois (for BRS
searches) and the University of Michigan (for LIS, SDC searches)
the fee covers maximum connect time per search and the requester
pays the vendor's rate for off-line printing. The fixed fee applies
to direct costs only at both universities. Michigan State University
(for BRS searches) and the University of Minnesota (for BRS and NLM
searches) include in their fixed fee a maximum number of off-line prints,
as well as maximum connect time. The fee at Michigan State University
covers some indirect costs. Michigan State University policy is based
on their past volume and connect time and reflects an average search time
of ten minutes at the terminal. While no maximum time is specified in
their policy, the fixed fee is nevertheless based on an anticipated time
of roughly ten minutes.

## Summary

With this general overview of the charging policies at the Big Ten universities, we will discuss some of the interesting policies implemented by a few of the libraries and will address some issues related to future use of on-line reference services.

Use of federal funds to support on-line reference services in academic libraries was found at both Ohio State University and Purdue University. However, unlimited use of the Information Bank is not permitted, and searchers screen the requests for appropriateness of topic. Ohio State University policy limits free usage to seven connect hours per month, and the library has not exceeded this limit. The LSCA project which funds the Information Bank at the Indiana State Library will end, after three years, in April 1978. Initially, there were no limitations imposed on search time or number of citations. However, with increased demand, a later policy imposed a limit on the number of citations. Complete evaluation of the project will appear in Library Occurrent, the professional journal of the Indiana State Library. A similar project is currently beginning which will provide access to LIS and SDC through Indiana local libraries. Requests will be sent to the state library for searching.

The University of Michigan library will be offering an inexpensive package to attract their undergraduate students. For $5.00 the requester can search one data base (ERIC, Psychological Abstracts, or Magazine Index), with a maximum of three terms, and receive a maximum of 15 on-line citations. This type of policy appears to be an innovative way to introduce a requester to the potential advantages of on-line searching. While many libraries provide free on-line demonstrations to introduce potential requesters, campuses with large populations probably cannot hope to apply this policy equitably. However, limited searches for which a nominal charge is made, may satisfy undergraduate students whose class projects may not require the more developed search strategy that is usually necessary for graduate student and faculty requests.

The evidence of networks is apparent where MIDLNET in particular has represented the University of Iowa and Northwestern University in negotiating a group contract with BRS. The motivation for participation in a consortium is the reduction of costs experienced by individual members who otherwise would incur high charges with separate contracts.

Most of those interviewed felt the library could not absorb an increased percent of the cost for on-line services. The indirect expenses (i.e., salary and training) were felt to be a strain on the library budget. In addition, good on-line searchers are in much demand, and, when offered better job opportunities, staff will move. Thus, high turnover in the staffing of on-line reference services adds an additional burden to the library budget.

By increasing the library's subsidization of these services, many felt that the library could not expand staff, and hence the budget, in order to meet increased demand. We found that library managers are not yet willing to replace abstracting and indexing journal subscriptions with purchase of on-line reference services. There are some major problems which must be resolved before library managers can realistically change their subscription policies. We can identify some of these problems as they relate to librarians, data base vendors, data base producers, and library patrons.

Possession of publications and number of volumes housed in a library should not inhibit quality of service and access to information. Ranking libraries by collection size ignores the primary function of libraries which is providing the requester with information and publications.

Libraries would experience increased demand if direct costs were entirely absorbed by their budgets. Because the burden of additional staff cannot be supported by library budgets, vendors must offer better designed interactive systems that can be used by the requester without an intermediary searcher.

Data base producers must be made aware of the retrieval requirements of requesters. If a data base does not completely correspond to the abstracting and indexing journal found in the library, the library patron may resist using the on-line service. For example, assume the on-line data base does not include the abstracts found in the corresponding printed journal or the abstract identification numbers. Without this useful information the library patron may have to retrace his or her search steps manually or spend many hours locating and evaluating many original articles that are only tangentially related to the primary interest of the study. The library patron will most likely judge the on-line reference service as unsophisticated and inefficient. Development of better interactive features for information retrieval systems is probably the problem that most discourages library managers from full financial support of on-line reference services.

In summary, the Big Ten universities are charging all or a portion of the direct costs to requesters. (Free searches of the Information Bank are made possible by federal funds and thus not totally subsidized by Ohio State University and Purdue University libraries.) Most of the Big Ten libraries absorb a portion or all of the indirect costs. Access to multiple vendors of data bases with different types of contracts usually results in multiple charging policies to the library patron. While most academic librarians probably believe that the library should provide access to information at no cost to the user, library managers of the Big Ten universities have in general decided that the current use of on-line reference services must be charged at least in part, to the requester. While the current environment may dictate charging library patrons for on-line reference services, we believe that future improvements in on-line systems will result in the library's absorbing an increasing percentage of the total cost. When on-line services become as widely accepted in the public services area of the library as they are in the technical services area, library patrons will expect tailored subject bibliographies to be as readily available as the classics in literature.

## Literature Cited

1.  "IROS at the University of Southern California." Journal of Academic Librarianship 3 (September 1977).

2. "Libs 100 Facilitates Networking In Illinois." CLSI Newsletter 2 (Fall 1976).

3. Williams, M. E. and S. H. Rouse. "Online Use of Data Bases in Illinois." Illinois Libraries 60 (April 1978): 429-35.

4. Williams, M. E. and S. H. Rouse. Computer Readable Bibliographic Data Bases - A Directory and Data Sourcebook. Washington, D.C.: American Society for Information Science, 1976.

5. Wanger, J., C. Cuadra and M. Fishburn. Impact of On-Line Retrieval Services: A Survey of Users, 1974-75. Santa Monica, CA: System Development Corp., 1976.

6. Williams, M. E. "Computer-Readable Data Bases," ALA Yearbook. Chicago: American Library Association, 1978.

7. Williams, M. E. "Computer-Readable Data Bases." ALA Yearbook. Chicago: American Library Association, 1977.

8. Cooper, M. D. and N. A. DeWath. "The Cost of On-Line Bibliographic Searching." Journal of Library Automation 9 (September 1976): 195-209.

# GETTING IN DEEPER AND DEEPER:
## USERS FEES FOR SERVICES AT THE MAYO CLINIC LIBRARY

by

Jack D. Key
and
Katherine J. Sholtz
Mayo Clinic Library

Medical librarians, with imagination and hard work, have accomplished much in resolving information management problems and have been doing so in economical ways. They have earned creditability in the eyes of their colleagues in medicine as a result of their achievements in this very special profession. Medical libraries, over the years, have changed and continue to change, and an important part of the profession is ensuring that this change is improvement. The factors of accountability are becoming increasingly evident, and it is apparent that future developments will be influenced greatly by the efficiency with which the information needs of users can be managed as well as by the cost savings that can be developed through continuous planning and modification.

What can libraries do today when faced with almost overwhelming demands for services from increasing numbers of patrons while operating on shrinking dollars in a field where prices continue to rise? There are few options. Certainly as everyday exigencies and growing challenges to service are faced, many factors must be addressed, not the least of which is operating expense. Some effective balance must be maintained between, on the one hand, mission, priorities, and traditions and, on the other, the dollars available to purchase materials, services, and whatever else is required to fill needs with available resources. At the Mayo Clinic, our intent is to continue to be conscientious stewards of each Clinic dollar used in library service, to be concerned with the efficiency of the library, and to be as cost-effective as possible with all services and activities. Our experience to date suggests that we have done well in accommodating the desire of the Clinic administration and the biomedical needs of our users to financial realities.

The chief purpose of the Mayo Clinic Library is to serve the Mayo programs of medical education, research, and health care by making biomedical literature readily available and by providing efficient assistance in its utilization. The library, established in 1907, contains more than 220,000 volumes that include historic medical writings as well as current project reports. The library provides adequate reference and research materials for all subject areas in medicine and science within the scope of the collection.

In addition to its primary clientele, the Mayo library serves visiting physicians, medical and allied-health students, professional persons such as lawyers and ministers, and individuals in the health-related sciences, as well as individuals and institutions participating in regional and national medicine-related programs.  Further, this library serves as one of the medical resource libraries in the nationwide Biomedical Library Network, which extends from the National Library of Medicine in Bethesda, MD, to 11 regional medical libraries, to resource libraries, and to basic medical units such as hospitals, small clinics, and individual health professions.  Essentially, the network provides orderly access to health science information for health-care professionals and educators who are not located near major medical centers.

All medical and hospital libraries are automatically part of the Biomedical Library Network.  If requested information is not available locally or at the nearest resource library, the request is relayed to the Regional Medical Library, to another region where the information is available, or, finally, to the National Library of Medicine.  Thus, any health professional has access to the nationwide network of medical library resources.

Network resource libraries, such as the Mayo Clinic Library, have made a commitment to regional development within the framework of the national network and have assumed responsibility for service to and coordination of a geographic area.  These libraries have been designated "resource" facilities because they have the resources, personnel, capacity, and dedication required to meet most service requirements for their states or areas.  They are widely active in the interlibrary loan program in their region and coordinate services to other health science libraries and to health sciences-related personnel within their own states or areas.

Services offered by resource libraries specifically and all health sciences libraries generally may vary but will generally include many, if not most, of the following:  reference (orientation and library user training programs, quick reference telephone service, interlibrary loans, bibliographic verification, literature searches and compilations of bibliographies--which may be manual or on-line computer retrievals of specialized subject information--and tailored selective dissemination of information services), services for hospitalized patients, reader services, photocopying, translations, staff bibliographies, book orders, field visits and consultations, library workshops, librarian education programs, exhibits, and patient health education.

These services are not intended to be one-way activities.  As far as possible, health professionals should meet their own specialized literature needs and should support basic up-to-date collections of books, journals, and reference material for their local hospitals and clinics.

The extension services of the Mayo Clinic Library are consistent with the aims of the Mayo Foundation in meeting its responsibilities as "a private trust for public purposes."  In this respect, our mission is to make the resources and services of the national biomedical information network and those of the Mayo Clinic Library reasonably accessible to health professionals.

Since 1970, we have charged for document delivery services--that is, non-clinic library users have been charged on a cost basis for any photocopies relating to interlibrary loans. In 1973, several other extension services were added to the "charge for" list: on-line computer retrievals of specialized subject information, field visits, library consultations, and library workshops.

In 1975 and again in 1977, we decided to look at all library services appropriate to fee-for-service arrangements for all users (Clinic and non-Clinic), to deliberate the questions of who should be charged and how much, and to implement what was possible after administration approvals. A formal detailed analysis was developed that identified each such appropriate service, level of activity, potential dollar amounts that would be recovered, and proposed charges reflecting all elements that should be included, such as staff time, machine time, equipment, supplies, indirect costs, and possible charge-back variations for different groups of users.

Limitations were noted as stipulations to our deliberations: fees for services must be consistent with both Clinic and library network commitments and philosophies; charges to users should be realistic and equitable and should conform to the philosophy of equal access; such charges should discourage frivolous use but should not impede legitimate need; the program should provide an appropriate degree of management control over the growth and use of library services, thus enabling the library to sustain the quality and performance of the services; the program must be flexible enough to permit periodic rate changes to reflect actual costs so that annual reviews could dictate automatic adjustments to the rate formulas; the fees collection system must be clerically simple; there must be some assurance that library resources would continue to provide equal and needed access to library services; and as far as possible, it would be desirable for the continued growth of services to users to be largely independent of the library budget.

Currently at this library, users are being charged for selected services. With few exceptions, charges are applied universally, and in all instances, the charge reflects actual unit costs based on formulas involving (where appropriate) staff time, machine time, equipment, supplies, postage, indirect expenses, and overhead expenses. Fees are charged to departmental accounts, to the individual user, or to institutions originating the work orders.

### Charged-Out Services

- Mediated photocopy. The Mayo Clinic Library complies with the provisions of the Copyright Revision Act of 1976 (PL-553).
- Interlibrary loans. Direct charges are imposed for interlibrary loans of "hard-copy" monographs and journals, for audiovisual programs, and for photocopied materials sent in lieu of originals. Some interlibrary loan activity is subsidized by the National Library of Medicine through the Regional Medical Library Network. There are also a number of quid pro quo exceptions.
- On-line computer data base searches. MEDLINE searches are provided free of charge to Mayo Clinic users, but all other users are charged. Searches using other data bases are charged back to the users.

- Update searches. Selective dissemination of information (SDI) update searches, performed at regular intervals, are charged to the users. If MEDLINE searches are involved, the service is charged out even to users at the Mayo Clinic.
- Manual literature searches related to extension activities.
- Translations.
- Librarian consultations and field visits related to extension services.
- Library training workshops. Registrations are charged to those participating in training workshops sponsored by extension services.
- Medical bookstore operated by Mayo Clinic Library. Any discount exceeding ten percent on book purchases for individuals or the bookstore, although not strictly speaking a fee-for-service, is retained by the library.

Levels of activity by year for selected services and total expense credits (fees) collected are presented in Figure 1. The amount of activity is given on a relative scale of values, the first year shown having been assigned a value of 1.00 for comparison. In most cases after a partial or complete charge was instituted, demand for the service did not decline.

Figure 1

Levels of activity related to expense credits
(fees) for selected Mayo Clinic Library services

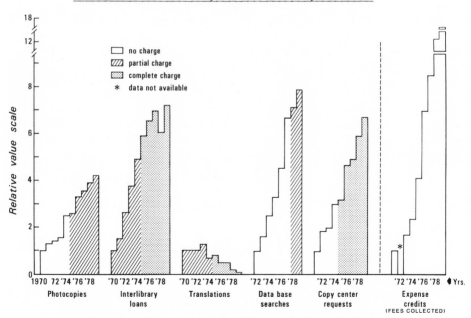

A review of photocopying within the library shows that since charges for some services were begun in 1974 and 1975 (a coin-operated machine for visitors and some students, mediated copying for the Clinic departments, and interlibrary loans), fees have been received for about 50% of the total activity.

Interlibrary loans have continued to rise despite the initiation of fees. The small reduction in requests for loans in 1978 was probably only partly due to increased charges. Reductions in the amounts reimbursed by the National Library of Medicine and changes in copyright law also may have had some impact.

Requests for translations have decreased steadily over the past few years, undoubtedly caused in part by the high cost of commercial translation services and also by the more widespread availability of English abstracts in foreign language journals.

Before 1978, fees for data base searches were assessed on a cost basis only to non-Clinic persons who made the requests. Receipts were negligible. Since early in 1978, the library has charged fees to user departments within the Mayo Clinic for commercial data bases. No fees are charged Clinic users for those data bases offered by the National Library of Medicine unless they are part of a continuing SDI search. A nominal monthly charge is assessed departments for SDI searches. Requests for National Library of Medicine data base searches and SDI searches continue to increase each year, even though the charges are assessed. A slight reduction in commercial searches has occurred this year.

Our copy center provides one copy of an article to an individual in lieu of charging out the journal; that way, material is retained in the library for use by other patrons. This service is in great demand, and its use increased significantly even after fees were imposed.

Since 1971, we have had almost an 18-fold increase in fees collected by the library for its services. Perhaps because these fees are assessed against the departments as part of their cost of providing a high, up-to-date level of care for patients, almost no objections are heard.

## Advantages of User Fees

Euphemistically termed "expense credits," the fees generated for our services have helped to ameliorate a growing and somewhat visible annual budget--charging distributes the expense of providing a service directly to the beneficiary of that service. In addition, allocating some or all of resource expenses to the user helps determine the real cost of an "overhead" service department, charging tends to moderate abuses in demands for services, and development of a charge system forces the library to analyze the purposes and sequences of activities and to study work-measurement. The results are a better understanding of the activities of the library and thus an increased awareness of the value of the library to the institution. Perhaps most important, charging fees allows the library, as well as the institution, to monitor its services. Production records are readily available for review and for the easy pinpointing of trouble areas. Records and statistics can help justify the hiring of additional personnel and the use of capital expenditures for new equipment. If the system is properly structured, the cost-effectiveness of a particular service should be readily apparent from the financial statements. Such cost-effectiveness can cause library personnel to become cost-conscious.

## Disadvantages of User Fees

The major negative feature of user fees is their depressant effect on those who are unprepared for them or who are less able to pay them. A person, department, or institution inadequately funded or conditioned may be reluctant to utilize needed services. Also, a tendency, which might be termed a disadvantage, is the accretion--and, if one is not careful, the inappropriate addition--of library services for which fees are demanded. We must keep in mind our raison d'être and keep necessity, priority, ability, and resources in wise balance. Lastly, a library receiving revenue from fees may find that the committee approving its budget seeks to reduce or eliminate allocations for the services.

## Postscript

In recent years, several measures, in addition to users fees, have been introduced to the Clinic, which collectively help reduce costs and improve income for library operations without compromising general strength or ability to perform. Selected examples follow.

- Some reductions were made in clerical personnel, with the remaining clerks assuming responsibility for split shifts to cover clerical functions in more than one department. We generally have been able to make more efficient and effective use of the total staff.
- Library orientation programs were begun for secretarial and paramedical employees. As knowledgeable library users, these individuals, when making routine use of the library, save valuable time of both librarians and those for whom they work.
- An OCLC on-line cataloging program was introduced in 1975, and to date it has far exceeded our original expectations. The amount of personnel time expended with OCLC to generate cataloging is much less than that used under the old system. OCLC has given us the opportunity to eliminate many procedures; the result has been economy in both manpower and time.
- A 3M Company Tattle-Tape theft detection system (with full-circulating mode) was installed in the library in early 1977. This detection system has proved to be cost-effective, provides a real deterrent to theft, and, perhaps more significantly, has lowered library patrons' frustration at being unable to find missing materials.
- A policy for lost or long-overdue books was developed to permit the library to charge persons who are not responsive to the needs of others or persons who deprive the library of money that could have been used for new books instead of for replacements.

These examples are representative of the measures we have taken to solve some of our problems. Others, to mention several briefly, include more specific guidelines for the acquisition of materials; systematic, continuous monitoring of the needs of users; annual analysis and purging of current titles and subscription lists; and task analysis of technical processing services recommendations. When fully implemented, the last-named measure will permit more efficient work-flow processing, better use of personnel through the elimination of duplicated tasks, and the merger of files for more economical management of records.

Medical information and services are not free--someone pays for them.  Future survival of the private library may depend in part on the ability to obtain remuneration for marketed information and services, to be cost-effective, and to communicate well the cost-benefits of what the library has to offer.  In any case, with our endeavors we hope not to lose sight of our role in the objectives of the organization of men and women known as the Mayo Clinic, Mayo Foundation, Mayo Medical School, and Mayo Graduate School of Medicine, collectively a "private trust for public purposes," which exists "to offer to both the sick and the well comprehensive medical care of the highest standard through a coordinated and integrated group practice of medicine."*  As far as possible, we will balance ability and resources with need.

Service is the basic commodity.  Patrons have a right to expect quality and timeliness for their payments.  In other words, library service must meet the test of worthiness.

---

*Mayo Board of Trustees and Board of Governors, _An Adventure in Medicine_ (Rochester, MN:  Mayo Foundation, 1970), p. 1.

# A BUSINESS PERSPECTIVE:
## OR, WHAT AM I DOING IN THE MIDDLE OF THIS DEBATE?

by

Faye Brill
Foote, Cone & Belding

User fees are being established by all sorts of libraries. Insufficient tax bases are causing administrators of publicly supported institutions to look at fees as a way to maintain or expand services. New types of businesses are being founded to do nothing but supply information or articles on demand, and for a fee. Corporate libraries, operating in a different environment, must develop a system for distributing their costs equitably. Even in a corporation, funds for a library are limited, and a correlation between tax supported institutions and corporate operating budgets does exist.

From a business perspective, somebody must pay for a corporate information center. Such a center is not producing sales, and therefore, is not contributing to profits directly. It is an invisible asset. Corporations usually require that divisions pay for the business and marketing information services directly or indirectly, or in combination. An indirect system of payments would be to include the service as corporate overhead. All divisions pay into corporate overhead expenses based on some formula, usually a percentage of sales or the number of employees. Information services would be a part of corporate expenses just like the president's salary, accounting, legal representation, and so forth. The budget for the center is subject to scrutiny as a proper proportion of the total corporate budget.

A second system would be for the center to charge according to use. Usually this system is based on a per-hour rate, requiring staff to keep strict records of how time is spent. The divisions are billed either on a per-job, monthly, or quarterly basis. Another system would be a combination of the two. As an example of a combined fee system, requests from divisions would be charged to the division, but services which are shared throughout the corporation would be corporate expenses. This system would ensure some sort of permanent budget for the services, while allowing users the opportunity to use the services whenever needed.

My experiences with two types of corporate settings illustrate two different user fee systems. At Ball Corporation, (Muncie, Indiana), where the information center had a staff maximum of three, we used the corporate overhead system. At Foote, Cone, and Belding (Chicago, Illinois), where the information center staff ranges from 12 to 15 members, a combination charge-back and overhead system is in effect.

At Ball Corporation, we decided in the very beginning, not to charge users directly--and this was a very deliberate decision.

Instead, the information center was to be part of corporate overhead and charge divisions annually on a percentage basis, based on each division's profits and sales. Thus, each of Ball's divisions would pay for the service regardless of use. Since the information center was a new concept at Ball, it needed to establish itself, and it needed time to provide worthwhile services. Most importantly, the center needed to develop a far-reaching public relations campaign just to let the divisions know of the center's existence. Ball had division head-quarters in several cities throughout the country, in addition to operating 21 plants. Each division would have to be told of the center's services. And while the services were "free" to divisions, use was encouraged.

As services were expanded to include newer methods such as on-line information retrieval, Ball still maintained a corporate overhead system for the divisions. The center was still in its infancy, espe-cially in its campaign to increase awareness of services in the divisions. For example, the best communicating device for me, as the manager of the center, was to visit each division to meet with the officers and managers who were most likely to use the services. These trips proved most effective. Immediately after a visit usage went up greatly and remained high. However, until all divisions were visited, and services explained, a direct usage fee system would have been unfair. Given the newness of the whole concept of information service, we had no choice but to charge each division a pro rata amount. This system resembles a tax for the public library, but of course, in a much smaller setting.

At Foote, Cone, and Belding (FCB), the situation was very differ-ent. FCB had had library services for years in three of its major domestic offices: Chicago, New York, and Los Angeles. However, when I joined the company, the decision had been made to consolidate infor-mation services in Chicago. Services would be expanded to include secondary research and analysis, and would be made available to all domestic and international offices.

FCB uses a combination of systems to cover the costs of operating the information center. An advertising agency exists to sell its advertising expertise, that is, to provide a client marketing services that would be difficult and expensive for a client to provide for itself. Advertising is a service oriented business. Payment for these services is the agency's income. Information center services form only a part of a package of agency services designed to result in profits. The quality of services FCB offers is used to distinguish that agency from a competing agency in convincing a client that it is better. This makes the information center visible and part of a very competitive business.

Since an advertising agency is reimbursed for providing services, the information center is just one of the operations for which the fees are appropriated. However, to confuse the issue more, the agency fee system does not directly correspond to information center fees. This is the result of the way requests are funneled into the center.

Routinely, clients request information from their account manage-ment group within the agency. It is the responsibility of account management to provide the information. Account management also must

rely on current information to oversee the total operation of developing for the client the best advertising campaign.  Usually this function
is divided among a number of agency departments, including media,
research, and creative.  Each department is responsible for its specialty.  Media determines the best communications medium in which to
place an ad (television, radio, consumer magazines, etc.).  Research
may be asked to find out how consumers view the product or to determine
whether there is a need for the product.  The creative department may
need to find out if the Beach Boys will allow one of its hit songs to
be used as a theme song.  Each department may request information from
the information center in order to perform its function for account
management.  In addition, account management may need a complete product
category history, answering such questions as:  what is the market size
for fish sticks, how many products exist in this category, what does
the literature say about the need for a new fish stick product, where
should we sell the product, and so forth.

This division of services will result in the advertising campaign.
The client is not paying each department directly for its part in
developing the campaign.  Rather, the client is paying the company for
the end result.  How the agency gets the end result is the agency's
business.  This illustrates, then, the structure of agency fees, but
does not directly relate to the fee structure of the information center.

The information center has developed an hourly rate to cover the
costs of providing services.  This rate is meant to cover the total
cost of operation of the center--including salaries, library materials,
on-line data bank services, replacement of equipment, rent, and so
forth.  When a request from any department is answered, the time spent
and the client are recorded, placing a dollar value on the information
provided.

As previously mentioned, FCB uses a combination of fee structures.
It uses a direct fee structure for some offices and an indirect
structure for others.  The large FCB offices, including those in New
York, Chicago, Los Angeles, and San Francisco, commit a percentage of
their client fees to the overhead of the center.  This system is similar
to the operation at Ball Corporation.  By participating in a percentage
system, each office can use the services of the center as much as it
wants without incurring additional fees.  To provide services to these
percentage offices equitably, the center is open 9 a.m. to 5 p.m. for
each office, or in Chicago terms, 8 a.m. to 7 p.m. daily.

Smaller FCB offices, which are actually subsidiaries, are billed
directly for use of the information center.  These bills are based on
the hourly rate mentioned before, and time is billed to the nearest
quarter hour.  Again, the hourly rate is established for all costs of
operating the center.  Separate segments are not billed directly (for
example, a data base search may take only 15 minutes, but the cost of
the search may be $30; the office is billed only for the 15 minutes,
which in this case would be lower than the center's actual cost).
Requests for information can be phoned in over the center's toll-free
number, or they can be placed by Telex or by mail.  The international
offices are also billed in this manner, and they usually place their
requests by Telex.

One purpose of the dual fee structure approach is to allow maximum benefits to all account management groups, and therefore, ultimately, the clients.  Subsidiary offices are offered the services of the parent company without having to pay for a service they may not need or may not be able to afford.  A subsidiary office could join the corporate overhead system if the benefits outweigh the costs to the subsidiary. Management is continually analyzing this possibility.  The system of fee structures also benefits the information center by ensuring that it has funds to afford the staff and resources it needs.  The service attempts to be comprehensive (in a large number of subject areas) and dependable.

This is an age of specialization as far as corporate information centers are concerned.  All specialize in the fields in which their corporations have an interest.  Requests to corporate centers, however, do not always fall within these areas.  The information center becomes a user of outside libraries at this point.

For myself, I would freely pay for information I needed to obtain from either another company or a public library.  At Ball Corporation, where the center was in its infancy, we would constantly need magazine articles, books, and other types of materials from other libraries. Occasionally I would need professional research and analysis.  It was my standard procedure to request articles from libraries which charged for supplying them.  Only in emergencies, when I needed the information the next day or when it was unavailable from a charging library, would I call a friend with a request.  My reasoning:  other corporate libraries were certainly too busy supplying information to their users to supply me with articles.  I felt that other company libraries that charged would have staffs dedicated to locating and providing articles I needed.

In most cases, corporate libraries can afford to pay for the services they need.  After all, the purpose of a corporate information center is to get as much information on as many subjects pertinent to that corporation in as small a space as possible.  The purpose is not to own everything, but to depend on outside services when necessary.

The following are some guidelines to providing corporate libraries information which a fee based service should consider:
1) The turn-around time must be fast--a week for a book or article should be sufficient.  Slower response makes the service practically worthless to a corporation.
2) The service must be reliable.
3) The price must be competitive.  The value of the service must outweigh the costs.  Should a service be perceived to be too costly, either go elsewhere, or purchase the item for the collection.  Should this perception be universal, the fee-based service may find itself without users.

Finally, eventually corporate libraries may all be pushed into charging our noncorporate clientele if we are taken advantage of--to protect ourselves from outside user's abuse.  An example of this was provided in the winter 1978 Business and Finance Division newsletter of Special Libraries Association, where a bank library in Canada had received and filled 2,911 interlibrary loan requests while requesting only 143 items in return.  The librarian in this situation had no alternative to establishing fees.

# FEES FOR SERVICE THROUGH INFORMATION BROKERS

# INFORMATION BROKERS

by

James B. Dodd
Georgia Institute of Technology


Individuals using large libraries provide custom services to business. Photocopies, proxy loans, literature searches are the main services. Legitimacy and purpose of free-lance operators are seriously questioned by some and lauded by others. What are the ethics, obligations, and rights of the libraries, the freelancers, and their clients?

In the early 1970s there surfaced in the world of libraries and information handling a method of operation that may ultimately have more impact on the profession than its present scope would indicate. This phenomenon is the growing number of independent information brokers who operate primarily as an interface between one or more libraries and paying information users. Their primary purpose is to make a profit.

Many of the users of today's information brokers are special libraries. But most of their clients are firms and individuals who do not have their own special library or do not use it.

This paper is an attempt to explore the problems and opportunities that exist and the ethics that need to be considered concerning the relationships that are developing among: 1) libraries, 2) information brokers, and 3) the clients of either or both.

The study grew out of extensive interviews with several information brokers, the staff of many of the libraries that they use, and industrial and business users of both the libraries and the information brokers.

By means of extensive interviews and conversations or a written questionnaire, 32 more or less viable information brokers have been contacted in the U.S. and Canada. Eighteen of them have made considerable contribution to this effort.

As for how many others there might be, this 32 may be of the same ratio as the tip is to the iceberg. My experience and statements from library staff members and from some of the brokers indicate that many companies have some arrangement with an outside individual that works with that company only. But these individuals are difficult to identify (1).

---

An Overview

An indication of the recency of this development is Davis's bibliography in which the earliest entry is 1969 (2).

Andrew Garvin, founder of Information Clearing House in New York with its better known subsidiary, FIND/SVP (3,4,5), estimates that the total private sector of information brokers is now a $5-$10 million dollar industry and that it will grow to ten times that size in ten years (6).

There are several terms, none totally accurate or satisfactory, which are used to try to label the group which is the subject of this study. Some of the terms are freelance librarians, information consultants, information specialists, and information-on-demand companies.

One practitioner said at a recent meeting that the designation, "Information-on-demand companies," is not very appropriate because clients do not demand much from them; they beat the bushes for clients (7). Too, information-on-demand is what every library should be ready to provide. One of the features that makes special libraries special is that they are information-on-demand organizations. Gaffner predicts that within ten years every library worthy of the name--special, public, academic--will be operating in an information-on-demand mode (8).

There are at least nine major academic and public libraries which have been operating active information-on-demand services as a regular part of the library for at least seven years. All of them certainly began as far back as the State Technical Services Act of 1965 and are continuing in operation on their own since the demise of that federal program (9,10,11,12).

The designation, "Independent Information Specialist," comes close to identifying the individual practitioner if not the service, except for one factor which is the source of many complaints and much friction: Some of the practitioners are not actually information specialists.

The term information broker (one who collects a fee for acting as an intermediary) will be used here as more nearly adequate to describe a service that they all have in common. However, this term incompletely describes most of the practitioners who bring considerably more professionalism and intellect to bear on their work than the simple transmission of information from one point to another.

The search for identity is also illustrated by the names under which the services operate. Note the permutations and combinations in their names of a group of common keywords: INFORM, Information Access, Information for Business, Information Specialists, Inc., Information Unlimited, International Information Service, Library and Information Service, Library Reports & Research Service, Inc., re·fer·ence, FIND/SVP, Editec, Inc., Document Transmission, Data Search Company, B.I. Associates, Telico.

Four recent articles (13,14,15,16) give detailed descriptions of the activities of different brokers. Here it will be sufficient to describe the various types briefly in order to establish the limits of the discussion.

## How They Operate

The simplest operation of the information broker is the single function of document delivery. The broker uses bibliographic expertise and bibliographic tools (his own or someone else's) to locate and obtain an original, or copy, of an item and deliver it to a user. Some brokers limit themselves to the use of a single large library, more frequently a university library. Others make use of any information resource accessible to them in a large metropolitan area. Some deal exclusively with government documents. They differ from the wholesalers and jobbers who must maintain massive operations within allowable discounts. These brokers deal in small quantities, usually single copies of an item; offer rapid, custom service; and charge a fee for their services above their cost for the document and out-of-pocket expenses. These document deliverers may be individuals working under the auspices of a large company in another sector of the information industry, or they may be a group of independent operators who are pooling their resources of time, know-how, and mobility.

At the other extreme are individuals, partnerships, and formally organized small corporations which undertake any project or assignment in the general field of information services. Many of these services go far beyond traditional library services--even far beyond services offered the most advanced special libraries. Some of the known services offered are document delivery (purchase, photocopy, or proxy loan); preparation of bibliographies; literature searches, manual and computerized; state-of-the-art reviews; handbook preparation; translations; library organization, development, and collection maintenance; information systems development, technical writing and editing; data collection and interpretation; location and referral to experts; assistance in the selection and hiring of library and information personnel; speech writing; indexing.

Paralleling the variety and scope of services offered by different brokers is the amount of involvement they have in their work. It is possible to work profitably as an independent information broker having made little or no investment in the business except for out-of-pocket expenses.

## How They Began

Some brokers began in simple opportunistic situations. For instance, one began a document delivery service as a means of adding to the family income at least long enough to help put a child through college. Another started a business as a moonlighting operation while employed as an industrial special librarian. Other individuals have been identified as doing literature searches on a moonlighting basis while employed in an academic library which operated an information-on-demand service to off-campus users.

Others have started into the business in a more forthright and direct manner after considerable thought and planning and, in some cases, with considerable investment and a willingness to take some risk.

One partnership began as the way out of a state of unemployment in an area oversupplied with trained librarians. At the time the librarian of the partnership could not locate a professional position, and the spouse of the other partner was suddenly out of work.

Another organization developed out of an acquaintence that began in graduate library school. By graduation the two students had decided to set up their own business in the information field and have gone on to a quite successful undertaking (13).

Some of the more aggressive information brokerage companies were not started by professional librarians. These companies tend to develop more specialized data bases in-house, to have made sizeable capital investments, and to have large staffs. Partly because of their size, visibility, and aggressiveness, and partly because of their use of untrained individuals, they also tend to be more frequently criticized by others in the library and information field.

Three issues need to be resolved, or at least considered, in the proper operation of the information broker in the information network: 1) conflict of interest, 2) fees to be charged and fees to be paid, and 3) the representation of someone else's work and expertise as one's own.

## Conflict of Interest

Conflict of interest is the least difficult of these problems to face, but the possibility does exist. In some cases the brokers themselves can be suspect of not being clear of conflict of interest. Examples are the industrial librarian who was moonlighting as a free lancer and the literature searcher working privately on the side instead of through the employer's literature search service.

In other cases the brokers may be encouraging conflict of interest problems in others. Some brokers maintain liaison with staff members at libraries who provide photocopies or loans from those libraries for the information broker. There are at least two possibilities for less than satisfactory activities: 1) the staff member may not limit the work provided to the broker to time outside the staff member's working hours, and 2) the staff member may pass along special privileges to the broker and his client in the way of reduced photocopy fees, special loan privileges, or other special treatment not generally available to outsiders.

## Fees

Since De Gennaro and others (17,22) cover the general topic of user fees for libraries and information services, these remarks will be limited to the fees paid by and to the information broker, specifically.

Many academic libraries charge outsiders a fee for borrowing privileges. When the broker, acting as agent for a number of companies, provides all those companies with the needed access to the library's collection by paying only one fee, the broker is depriving the library of some income and at the same time putting an additional burden on the library.

Especially in the public libraries there may be resentment because the broker is charging a fee for something that the client could have obtained free if the client had contacted the library directly. The

broker's response, of course, is that the client is paying for information that he did not have:  the client did not know to contact the
public library directly.  It is not the broker's fault that the client
did not know where to go to get the information free.  But is it proper
for the broker to withhold that knowledge from his client?  Many of the
sample search questions on the brokers' advertising lists would have
been answered without cost by the reference department of the public
library in any medium-sized city.

Many of the brokers list private corporate libraries and privately
supported special libraries among the resource centers they use.  The
spirit of special librarianship is built upon the willingness to
cooperate in depth with other librarians with almost no questions
asked.  But many of these special libraries, as indeed many public
libraries and many academic libraries, depend upon broad industrial
support in order to maintain their collections and offer special
services.  Can one really expect the staff and administrators of these
libraries to be happy when potential supporters are charged a fee for
resources of a library when none, or very little, of the fees accrue
to the library?

## Misrepresentation

Another criticism of some of the brokers is lack of know-how or
the selling of someone else's know-how or someone else's work as their
own.  Many cases were reported of individuals obtaining considerable
reference assistance (not just directional guidance) from the professional staff of a library, and then charging a client a consultant-type
fee for providing the information.  The truth is that if the individual
had not received help from the reference staff he might never have
found the information.

As indicated earlier, some of the brokers are not information
specialists.  The reference librarians and the public service staff
of some of the libraries they use are the real specialists.  The fact
that fees are charged is not the real source of resentment.  It is
that the fee does not contribute to the development of the basic
resource.  The proper fees are not collected by the library which
hires the real specialists.

## A Healthy Phenomenon

The foregoing may seem a bit harsh on the information brokers;
however, it is not the intent here to condemn all the brokers for all
their activities.  There is little subterfuge, and there is certainly
nothing illegal about obtaining all the free service one can from the
public library.  Who gets what kind of service is a problem for the
administrator and not for the broker.  Stated more positively, the
burgeoning of successful information brokers is a healthy occurrence.
They are showing what can be done with innovation, creative thinking,
and publicity or advertising (18,19).  They will also help to bury the
incorrect concept that library service is free.  It is not free--
"There's no such thing as a free lunch" (20).

Chanaud (14) and Klement (21) state the source of the cost

differently, saying that information is free, but that access to it is not free. In either case, the availability of information need not be expensive. What is expensive is the lack of information or at least the lack of the correct information. Both the well-informed business person and the poorly informed, frightened business person are willing to pay well to avoid the greater expense of doing without needed information.

There are several positive factors about the operations of the information broker.

First, most of them are capable of and usually do give good serv-ice. One of their critics said, "Of course they give good service. That is all they have." But, in the information business, if you have something else and do not give good service, you are not in the information business.

It is essential to the survival of the broker that he be able to respond quickly and effectively. One of the brokers said that if the client were not satisfied with what he received from the broker, he would not return for additional service. On the other hand, the staff member of a public or academic library can afford an occasional unhappy client, for there is the certainty that there will be new clients tomorrow. (This is true only within limits, as library users become more sophisticated and demanding.) But the results of poor service will more quickly affect the broker than they will the institutional staff member who will likely get paid at the end of the month, regardless of the service he supplies.

## Keys to Good Service

The brokers have the ability to give good service because they can be flexible. They do not have to make a large capital investment that needs to be used to be justified. Someone else has made the capital investment in the resources in the libraries to which they have access.

This flexibility is based on mobility. They are able to move from source to source. In the institutional library, on the other hand, the staff is usually confined to the limits of the institution. Such types of resource sharing as interlibrary loan do exist. But how frequently can or will a library staff member travel across town or even across campus to use a bibliographic tool not in his own library? To ask the other library to use that tool for him is almost unthinkable.

The broker can reply with a speed that is hard for the institu-tional library staff member to muster on a continuing basis. The broker knows what speed his client requires and responds accordingly. The broker also knows that the client is willing to pay for the cost of the speedy service, whether it is a long distance telephone call, special air freight delivery service, or a special trip across town or flight across the country to obtain the information.

While one possible negative factor about brokers could be their lack of know-how or their willingness to take advantage of someone else's know-how, the opposite is also true. Many are experts at locating and using information. They are inquisitive and flexible of mind as well as of movement. They are open minded and alert to new ideas and opportunities.

Their flexibility and speed also derives from their lack of
encumbrance with institutional and governmental red tape.

## Whose View?

How do the brokers view themselves, and how do others see them?
As one might expect, the brokers, like most of us, view themselves
quite favorably. None of those interviewed or who responded to the
written inquiry was the least bit critical of their means of operation.
Their view, simplified, is that they are performing a needed service,
doing it well, and are having little difficulty with the libraries and
other sources that they use.

But all is not happy in the relationships between the brokers and
the libraries that they use. Some hints of discord have appeared in
the literature recently (14).

The situations vary from: 1) a near symbiotic relationship
between the library and the broker, 2) to impositions and intrusions
by the brokers on the libraries, or 3) to the "let somebody else do it,
we don't want to be bothered" attitude, and 4) to the incapabilities of
some libraries to do the job no matter how sincerely they would like to.
Comments from the librarians on the staff of some of the libraries that
the brokers use indicate some approval and some disapproval of the
brokers' operations.

Some libraries welcome the presence of the broker in the library
because it keeps many nuisance clients out of the library. In other
situations the library staff members are unhappy, resentful, or perhaps
even jealous or envious of the brokers using their facilities. Some
brokers do demand free professional help from the staff. Some of them
provide less than satisfactory service. Some of them may be careless
about their use of the collection and may be inconsiderate of the rights
and needs of other users of the library.

In one area where there is a cluster of independent brokers, one
of them remarked that they, "are operating in the face of a great
institution that cannot get itself together." That institution, a
major university library, is so departmentalized and its collection so
scattered that the most effective network operating among the departments and branches is made up of the independent brokers who move freely
from one collection to another to use the reference tools or to make
photocopies with a speed and versatility that the giant library system
cannot accomplish by itself. In this type of case, part of the normally
internal circuitry of the information network has been externalized with
a sort of bypass valve.

## What Would You Do If . . .?

In an effort to place the work of the independent brokers in
perspective, consider these questions.

- ° Would you, as a company librarian, use the services of a free-
  lance operator to obtain photocopies of material which you know
  to be located in a specific library? Why should you? Why
  shouldn't you? Why not go directly to the library?
- ° Would you, as a special librarian, utilize the services of an

independent operator to locate material for you when you have no
way of determining the location of the material on your own?
Why should you? Why shouldn't you?

° Would you, as the interlibrary loan librarian in an academic
library, utilize the service of a free-lance operator to obtain
copies of materials known to be in another university library
when you know that the other interlibrary loan service is very
slow or when the only way to verify, and thereby sanctify, the
reference is to go look at the volume itself?

° How would you respond, as a reference librarian on the staff of
a college library, to a lawyer friend who offers to pay you to
spend an evening or two or your weekend locating some articles
to strengthen one of his cases? Would you recognize the opportunity and would you initiate the suggestion that you should be
paid for your professional know-how?

° Consider the same situation, except that you are in the cataloging department of that college library. Next, promote your-
self to head librarian and judge if your reaction might be
different. What would you do in the same situation if you were
on the staff of a public library?

° Suppose you are the research librarian in a medium-sized manufacturing firm or in an advertising agency and a neighbor--an
engineer or a salesman--tells you that he needs to use a library
once in a while but just does not have the time to do it. What
would you tell him?

## Filling a Need

No one disagrees with the basic need for libraries and for the
development of library services. But if libraries are not capable, or
not adequately supported with funds, or do not wish to deliver these
special services, then some other agency needs to step in and do it.
That is basically what the information brokers are doing.

There exists a partial vacuum, an unnatural phenomenon, and the
pressure is being somewhat relieved by a new type of service. In the
spirit of entrepreneurship or with a need to make a living, some enter-
prising spirits have recognized a need and an opportunity and are making
efforts to fill that need.

Nobody should interfere with a person's right and capability to
make a profit (or a living) selling a product in a free market in this
country. Perhaps it has already been recognized that information is a
marketable product, and that tax-supported libraries have been rele-
gated to the level of a welfare agency which doles out information at
no cost to those who cannot afford to pay for it.

The information brokers, along with other network participants,
need to give themselves close scrutiny and must work to find each one's
proper place in the overall information network so that the cost of the
network is supported in proper proportion by all who use it, so that it
works equally well for all those who need it, and so that it not be
short-circuited.

Only one thing is certain. This is an area of librarianship in
which the rules, regulations, and codes have not been established. The

profession is breaking away from concepts and methods of operation to which unquestioning adherence has become a manacle.

While iron-clad rules and regulations for the information brokers to follow are not necessary, there is a need for something more than the caveat emptor approach. Using the guidance, support, and discussion that can take place within a professional organization, there is an opportunity for the Special Libraries Association to foster the development of standards against which the information-on-demand organizations, both private and institutional, academic and public libraries included, can measure their performance and the quality of their services.

## Acknowledgments

The author especially wishes to thank the information brokers who have talked to him and written openly and frankly about their operations.

## Literature Cited

1. Fromberg, Katherine / Private Communication Concerning University of Southern California. Edward L. Doheny, Jr. Memorial Library's Industrial Associate Library Survey, 1975.

2. Davis, Maxine W. / A Quick Guide to Free Lance Librarianship. Wilson Library Bulletin 49 (no. 6):445 (Feb 1975).

3. Fearon, Robert / FOUND: One Answer to the Information Explosion. Madison Avenue 16 (no. 3):12-14 (Mar 1973).

4. Doebler, Paul / "Seek and Ye Shall FIND." Publishers Weekly 202 (no. 16):39-42 (Oct 16, 1972).

5. Find: Information on Demand. Burroughs Clearing House 58 (no. 1):30, 64, 66 (Oct 1973).

6. Garvin, Andrew / Panel: Information-on-Demand Companies: Problems and Prospects. American Society for Information Science Annual Meeting, Atlanta, Oct 15, 1974.

7. Warner, Alice Sizer / Panel: Information-on-Demand Companies: Problems and Prospects. American Society for Information Science Annual Meeting, Atlanta, Oct 15, 1974.

8. Gaffner, Haines B. / Information-on-Demand Services: Progress to 1975--Forecast to 1985. Information Industry Association Information Marketplace Luncheon, Mar 5, 1975.

9. Shannon, Zella J. / Public Library Service to the Corporate Community. Special Libraries 65 (no. 1):12-16 (Jan 1974).

10. Dodd, James B. / "Pay-As-You-Go Plan for Satellite Industrial Libraries Using Academic Facilities." Special Libraries 65 (no. 2):66-72 (Feb. 1974).

11. Henkle, Herman H. / The John Crerar Library: a Complex of Special Collections and Special Library Services. Illinois Libraries 45:509-512 (Nov 1963).

12. Wood, Frances K. / KNOW (Knowledge Network of Wisconsin) and ISD (Information Services Division). Special Libraries Association. Contributed Papers Sessions, 66th Annual Conference, Chicago, Jun 8-12, 1975. Microfiche. Illinois Chapter, Special Libraries Association, Chicago, Ill.

13. Warner, Alice Sizer / ?&! Information Services: New Use for an Old Product. Wilson Library Bulletin 49(6):440-444 (Feb 1975).

14. Chanaud, Jo and Robert Chanaud / The Independent Information Specialist and the Research Library. Society of Research Administrators Journal 6 (no 3):26-31 (Winter 1975).

15. Monson, Gordon, Jr. / Coping with the Demand. American Libraries 6 (no. 2):72 (Feb. 1975).

16. Goodfellow, Marjorie E. / Library Consulting: A View from Quebec. QLA Bulletin 16 (no. 2):3-6 (Apr-May-Jun 1975).

17. De Gennaro, Richard / Pay Libraries & User Charges. Library Journal 100 (no. 4):363-367 (Feb 15, 1975).

18. Hirsch, Annette / Panel: Information-on-Demand Companies: Problems and Prospects. American Society for Information Science Annual Meeting. Atlanta, Oct 15, 1974.

19. Services Available. Food for Thought (Food Librarians Division, SLA) 6 (no. 4):71 (Jan 1975).

20. Kingman, Nancy M. / The Special Librarian / Fee-Based Interface, or There's No Such Thing as a Free Lunch. Special Libraries Association. Contributed Papers Sessions, 66th Annual Conference, Chicago, Jun 8-12, 1975. Microfiche. Illinois Chapter, Special Libraries Association, Chicago, Ill.

21. Cheda, Sherrill / The Free-lance Alternative in Librarianship: An Interview with Susan Klement. Canadian Library Journal 30:401-406 (Oct-Nov 1973).

22.  IIA Urges User Fees for Libraries in NCLIS Testimony.  American Libraries 4 (no. 6):333 (Jun 1973).

23.  WLB's Minidirectory of Information Specialists.  Wilson Library Bulletin 49(6):442 (Feb 1975).

# BIBLIOGRAPHY

# USER FEES BIBLIOGRAPHY

This bibliography is intended to provide the reader with a list of key materials on the subjects of user fees in libraries and user fees for other public services. The list is not exhaustive and should be used as an entry point to materials in the field. The inclusion of materials related to user fees in general and user fees for specific public services is intended to give a broader perspective and context for consideration of user fees in libraries.

American Library Association. Charging for Computer-Based Reference Services. Edited by Peter G. Watson. Chicago: American Library Association, 1978.

American Library Association. The Information Society: Issues and Answers. American Library Association's Presidential Commission for the 1977 Detroit Annual Meeting. Edited by E. J. Josey. Phoenix, AZ: Oryx Press, 1978.

Baumol, William J., and William G. Bowen. Performing Arts: The Economic Dilemma. New York: The Twentieth Century Fund, 1966.

Bhatt, Kiran, et. al. Congressional Intent and Road User Payments. Washington, D. C.: The Urban Institute, 1977.

Blake, Fay, and Edith Perlmutter. "Libraries and the Market Place," Library Journal 99 (January 15, 1974): 108-111.

Blake, Fay, M., and Edith L. Perlmutter. "The Rush to User Fees: Alternative Proposals," Library Journal 102 (October 1, 1977): 2005-2008.

Casper, Cheryl. "Library Pricing Models and Information Requirements: A Case Study." Ph.D. dissertation, Case Western Reserve University, 1975.

Casper, Cheryl A. "Subsidies for Library Services," Encyclopedia of Library and Information Science. New York: Marcel Dekker, to be published.

Chen, Ching-Chih, et. al. Citizen Information Seeking Patterns: A New England Study. Executive Summary Report for the White House Conference on Library and Information Services. Boston: Simmons College of Library Science, 1979.

"Cities are Being Forced to Change Fiscal Policies and Services in the
1980's," Wall Street Journal (October 24, 1979): 5.

Cooper, Michael D. "Charging Users for Library Service," Information
Processing and Management 14 (1978): 419-27.

Cooper, Michael D., and Nancy A. DeWath. The Cost of On-Line
Bibliographic Searching. Stanford, CA: Applied Communication
Research, 1975. Technical Report ACR-003-75-01.

Crawford, Paula J., and Judith A. Thompson. "Free Online Searches are
Feasible," Library Journal 104 (April 1, 1979): 793-95.

Domencich, Thomas A., and Gerald Kraft. Free Transit: A Charles River
Associates Research Study. Lexington, MA: D. C. Heath, 1970.

Drinan, Helen. "Financial Management of Online Service - A How-To
Guide," Online 3 (October 1979): 14-21.

"The Economics of Academic Libraries." Edited by Allen Kent, Jacob
Cohen, and Leon Montgomery. Library Trends 28 (Summer 1979).

Feldstein, Kathleen F. "The Economics of Public Libraries." Ph.D.
dissertation, Massachusetts Institute of Technology, 1976.

Forecasting International Ltd. Potential Impacts of Automation and
User Fees Upon Technical Libraries. For the National Science
Foundation. Springfield, VA: National Technical Information
Service, 1977. PB 271418.

Friedman, Milton. "Introduction: Playboy Interview," in There's No
Such Thing as a Free Lunch (LaSalle, Ill.: Open Court, 1975),
p. 1-38.

Gell, Marilyn K. "User Fees I: Economic Argument," Library Journal
104 (January 1, 1979): 19-23.

Gell, Marilyn K. "User Fees II: The Library Response," Library
Journal 104 (January 15, 1979): 170-73.

Giuliano, Vincent E. "A Manifesto for Librarians," Library Journal
104 (September 15, 1979): 1837-42.

Goddard, Haynes, C. "An Economic Analysis of Library Benefits,"
Library Quarterly 41 (July 1971): 244-55.

Highway Trust Fund and Federal Aid Highway Financing Program. Hearings before Committee on Ways & Means. U.S. House of Representatives, 86th Congress, 1st session. Washington, D. C.: July 22, 23, 24, 1959.

Hirshleifer, Jack. "Economics of Information: Where are We in the Theory of Information," American Economic Review 63 (May 1973): 31-39.

Hirshleifer, Jack. "The Private and Social Value of Information and the Reward of Inventive Activity," American Economic Review 61 (September 1971): 561-74.

Huston, Mary, M. "Fee or Free: The Effect of Charging on Information Demand," Library Journal 104 (September 15, 1979): 1811-14.

Kalba, Kas. "Libraries In The Information Marketplace," in Libraries in Post-Industrial Society, edited by Leigh Estabrook (Phoenix, AZ: Oryx Press, 1977, p. 306-320.

Kranich, Nancy. "Fees For Library Service: They Are Not Inevitable!," Library Journal 105 (May 1, 1980): 1048-51.

McKenzie, Richard B., and Gordon Tullock. The New World of Economics. Homewood, IL: Irwin, 1975.

National Commission on Libraries and Information Science. Public Libraries: Who Should Pay the Bills. Washington, D. C.: NCLIS, 1978.

Newhouse, Joseph P., and Arthur J. Alexander. An Economic Analysis of Public Library Services. Lexington, MA: Lexington Books, 1972.

Swanson, Don R. "Libraries and the Growth of Knowledge," Library Quarterly 49 (January, 1979): 3-25.

U. S. Civil Aeronautics Administration. A Program of Charges for the Use of the Federal Airways System. Washington, D. C.: U. S. Department of Commerce, 1953.

Weaver, Frederick S., and Serena A. Weaver. "For Public Libraries the Poor Pay More," Library Journal 104 (February 1, 1979): 352-55.

Wharton, Clifton R. Jr. "Higher Education: Who Benefits, Who Pays?," Vital Speeches of the Day. 45 (October 1979): 744-46.

White Lawrence, J. The Dilemmas of the Public Library. New York: New York University, Faculty of Business Administration, 1978. Working Paper Series #78-86.